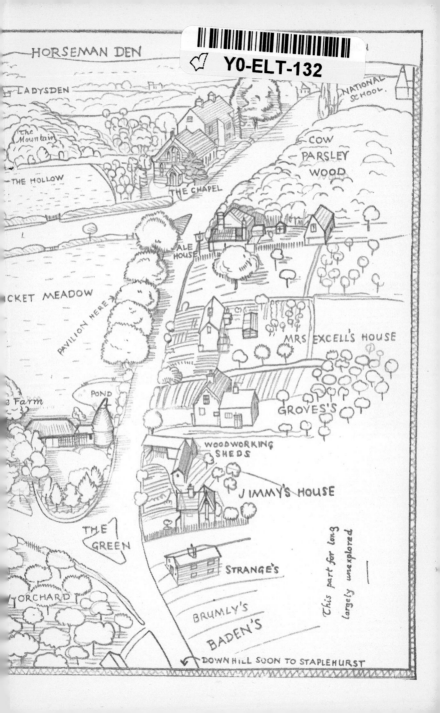

THE SMALL YEARS

THE SMALL YEARS

BY

FRANK KENDON

✻

With an Introduction by
WALTER DE LA MARE

CAMBRIDGE
AT THE UNIVERSITY PRESS
1950

PUBLISHED BY
THE SYNDICS OF THE CAMBRIDGE UNIVERSITY PRESS

London Office: Bentley House, N.W. 1
American Branch: New York

Agents for Canada, India, and Pakistan: Macmillan

First Edition June 1930
Reprinted July 1930
Reprinted with alterations December 1930
'Miscellany' edition 1937
Second Edition 1950

Printed in Great Britain at the University Press, Cambridge
(Brooke Crutchley, University Printer)

I DEDICATE
THESE PLEASANT MEMORIES
TO MY FATHER

CONTENTS

"That which was from the beginning, which we have heard, which we have seen with our eyes, which we have looked upon, and our hands have handled of the word of life. For the life was manifested, and we have seen it, and bear witness."

INTRODUCTION

" The memories contained in this book," says Mr Frank Kendon himself, and far too modestly, "are not much, but they are something which the world could not have without me. If I was luckier in my earth than many thousands, I am but trying to leave them the shadowy form of my joys, to wrestle with the angel of childhood till he tells me his secret." On the page that follows this there are references, lit with the light of the imagination, to the cuckoo, to snow, and then to the furtive childish rapture of stealing raspberries and gooseberries in a garden, creeping smally there among the bushes in that chequer of sun and shadow of the twigs and leaves— "and your hand going in among them." And these last seven words alone would be proof that he has not wrestled in vain. They tell of a secret something which is of a child's experience only and which is as clearly a divination of "the small years" as is his statement that "It is terrible to be in an ecstasy of joy, alone." And so again, in the passage that tells of his first enraptured glimpse of the blue of the succory flower—"I am partly what I am, even to-day," he says, "because I found it then, *with my eyes for my spirit*.... I am sure that the very fact that I remember it proves that it nourished life in me, and is part of me and indestructible."

Mr Kendon's book is an account, then, of the first few years of his childhood, a childhood seen in the retrospect of about thirty years. It is extraordinarily vivid and abundant, but even those of us whose glimpses of our "angel infancy" are far fewer and less vivid than his would agree that a light and intensity and a simple richness of being were ours then which is rare indeed in later life, and that we look back on those early days across a blue rift, as it were, of air and time—that an abyss divides us from them. The spirit within returns in glimpses thither as if to a world of dream. What causes that abyss?

It appears to be true, at any rate, that the childhood of a poet, as it is described by Mr Kendon, though it may differ in degree of delight and rapture, does not differ in kind from the childhood of other men. And reading such a book as this we realise that it is not the world of childhood which has changed, but that our attention and desire and interest have changed. It is *we* ourselves who are to blame, if blame there be. We realise also that in those far days we did not "measure distance by length but by remoteness, not by how far we had to go or had come, but by how far away we felt"; that we were surrounded when alone by a "wall of solitude," that we could at any happy moment "step down out of the sun into the dream," but that none the less "the smallness of our world could not shut us out of the world's immensity." What we remember too is not merely anything in itself, not merely as we lay in bed, thinking over the day that was gone, "a snowy scene, with children running, and sudden falls of fallen snow from pine-tree branches waving in the wind," but "the soul of a lovely experience agitating with delight the soul of a little boy falling asleep."

Such memories on the other hand, however precious to the possessor of them, may be neither striking nor significant. They are merely "little detached pieces of a jig-saw puzzle." They rise to the surface of memory quiet as a bubble, and lo, "within the limits of a lost moment," we are children again. Still, detached pieces though they may be, the complete puzzle was actually there if only we could find it, and it is not the same puzzle that lies before us now.

Mr Kendon was in love with life in the few years that closed the nineteenth century, and he falls in love with it again in looking back on them. Fears are told of, with an occasional glimpse of horror or of an unintelligible yet divinable evil. But these are few, and the passage on page 47 which describes the journey of a child from actuality into the state of sleep is untinged with fear at all. Indeed it is a condition of the mind worth a king's ransom.

Nor is it merely the plums of childhood that in memory taste so sweet. A curious delicious flavour may haunt even its duff. The commonest objects—a cupboard, a mug, a slice of cake, a door-bell, an old rocking-horse, a picture on a wall, the light reflected from snow, an old man's beard, his alpaca coat, the white of his eyes as he knelt praying—such things as these were somehow more themselves and therefore more enthralling. And it is not merely that growing older has bestowed on them a glamour evoked by time, envy and regret. Like runes scribbled on some grey old mouldering pre-historic stone, they had a secret meaning, though what precisely that meaning was we may not be able to say.

So too with the inspiration of that singular game, Let's pretend. As Mr Kendon says, the child himself is not deceived by it, however deeply submerged in it he may be. His nursery horse is a *wooden* horse, and the rain that floods out of the skies on the adventurer as he gallops into the dark on and on and on is never in any sense *real* rain to him. He is not in the throes of an illusion. For "The child can see the two worlds side by side and seriously live at once by two standards," whereas "the grown-up...doesn't pretend at all without either deceiving himself (when he is insane) or shamefastly laughing."

So too of a child's experiments in drawing —with his paint-box and its entrancing gamboge and prussian blue and crimson lake. Surely page 59 affords us not only a most illuminating insight into this childish state of mind which should be of sovereign help to the teacher—"childish pictures are rubbish to children"—but also gives every artist something essential to think about.

And how about Mr Kendon's old grandfather, who set up school in a barn, his charge twopence a week for every child that attended it, girl or boy? He had no theories; he was not a born teacher; but he knew what opportunities arise when a child is merely learning to read, to spell and to count. Without perhaps even realising it yourself you may—having the gift of so doing—at the same time and in the interstices, so to speak, teach him "to pray, to be kind, to be clean and neat, to be methodical and serious... and without extra charge you may teach him to grow up." We cannot but agree with Mr Kendon that this solemn, upright and zealous old man would have dismissed much of the wild experimental education of to-day as "mischievous nonsense." And it is as well at least to ask ourselves if he was right.

Quite apart, too, from the grown-up company to be shared in the following pages, and that company seen with the eyes of a child—a gallery as lifelike as it is various—we share the child's rapture in the life of nature, and the appalling first revelation of the tenuity of that life. A catapult and a shrilling wren in a plum tree thirty yards away: "We gasped with amazed laughter, and ran to the wren.

Its little entrails lay shining in the hot sun. Its eyes were shut, its beak was caught in the act of crying...and certainly it was dead—still—small—harmless—and brotherly, we suddenly saw. There was a pain at the back of my mind, as though something shameful had been done, and the day not shamed by it." It is an experience that has probably happened to every one of us, and at any rate brings back to my mind a little privy solitude of nearly fifty years ago, and that of a dusty morning in June. A pebble round as one of David's, and, for Goliath, a sparrow. Was it indeed a full twenty yards away—pecking there in the dust of the road? A marvellous shot! And then the hot, pallid, grinding shame of it.

But an introduction to a book—and immodest indeed must the introducer be who does not realise both the privilege and dangers of his little office—is intended to introduce, and not, however sharp the temptation afforded, to quote *ad infinitum*. He is bound to be an interloper between book and reader, but he need not be wearisome.

If, however, a last personal word be admissible, the reading of *The Small Years* has reminded me first—sobering thought—that though Mr Kendon writes as a grown-up, I am myself of an earlier generation than he is; and next, that being so, many of what were pure charms and magics to him in his early life— the mechanical separator in his aunt's dairy, for example, or the touching of a button that suddenly flooded the surrounding gloom with an electric blaze of light—are for me the very reverse of what in looking back they now seem to him. And this simply because they came into my world when I was more or less an adult and no longer a child!

I look back with a fond romanticalness to a one-horse 'bus with its little square skylight, its inner leather strap to its door, the immensely old ladies within it, nearly suffocating me in their skirts, and its straw to keep the feet warm. A grown-up of thirty years hence will be looking back with a like fond romanticalness to *his* first ecstatic and bewildering flight in a *Moth*.

This deceitful world may change, then— though may be not much in its spots. But the immortal child in man lives on. He lives on in a chequered paradise which for want of a better word we might as well call Eden. Alas, how few of us can recapture it—and how very few indeed with Mr Kendon's lovely truth and clarity. None the less we may remind ourselves that all the children of the world are to some degree sharers in that garden *now*, at this very moment. We can at least then attempt to refrain from being the self-appointed cherubims with flaming swords turning every way in an entirely unintentional effort to drive them out.

WALTER DE LA MARE

The Hill

I WAS born in 1893, the third child to my father and mother, at a boarding school for boys. The school stands on the crown of a small round hill rising in the middle of the Weald, and its playing fields and pastures and woodland all belonged to my grandfather, nearly fifty acres altogether of the homeliest sort of English country land, a kindly piece of England to be cradled in.

Three miles away a railway skirted our kingdom and led to London and so to all the world with which books were filled. Our very remoteness made us a world to ourselves: we were as self-supporting as civilization would allow; my father bought flour by the sack and coal by the fifty tons; but our gardens could keep us in potatoes; and we often had some of last year's apples still to eat in this year's May. As children we knew next to nothing of a reputed world; the kingdom of our wanderings was not ten miles across, and the kingdom of our eyes, from one horizon to the other, not more than twenty in the clearest weather; but these two circles encompassed enough to occupy all our faculties, until one by one we grew foolishly ambitious. Our neighbours were the original salt of the earth; and though meadows were our counties, and parishes our nations, our little world was quite large enough to get lost in. Ulysses could say no more.

From our nursery window you looked out above a laurel hedge which was all that separated the house from a road running north and south immediately below you. On the top of the orchard bank opposite grew elm trees, whose tops were so high that you had to stoop at the low window to see them against the sky. The morning sunlight came across the orchard, through the brushwood of the elms, and shone deep into the nursery till eleven or so, when it began to burn on the road. Looking down the hill to the right out of the window, you saw the long face of the school, from which a buzz of study came up; and lower down five graceful leaning ash trees, brothers, all worn smooth by many attempts to climb them. Past these playground trees the narrow road wound steeply down for half a mile, bordered with oak trees and a wood; and this was the way to Gowdhurst, the village where the church was. The name was on our letters, but the village was really a long way off, and it stood on a hill over against us to the south, but higher than our hill. There was a stile in the wall of the playground from which you could look over the playing fields, past the edge of our hill and across the semicircular valley of Combourne to the Gowdhurst hill, which was the boundary of our sight that way. High on the top among its trees the church tower stood, and though it was more than two miles away the air was generally so clear and bright (or so I remember it) that sharp eyes could distinguish the flag-staff set on the tower there.

Hundreds and thousands of trees filled the valley and hung about the hillsides; the horizon was rough with their round shapes; and where little runlets made their ways down the hill to join Combourne stream, great dark folds of woods covered them in. From northwest, by south, and round to the east, our knoll was thus walled in by hills and trees: towards the east there was a great wood called Old Park Wood, which ran all along the hillside. It was possible to go into this wood by Gowdhurst and to come out at Hor-Den, walking on moss under cover of trees the whole way without crossing a road or passing a house, three miles or more. It is true that there were hop-gardens, pastures, cornfields and orchards also on the sides of these hills; but orchards and hop-gardens, in summer at least, have their bowers like the woods, and all the short smooth sweeps of pasture were shaded by their own trees too, isolated giants of a whispering army.

3

All this lay south of an imaginary line drawn through our nursery window from the place of sunrise to that of sunset.

Put a little heap of sand in the middle of a saucer, but not so high as the edges of the saucer, reduce yourself to insect size, and build a school and a dozen cottages upon the heap of sand, cover sand and the south slopes of your saucer with trees in scale—you can hardly plant too many—and there in little you have my world at five; the southern half of it exactly true. But not the northern: on that side, though you cannot see it from the window, the saucer must be broken.

Looking north from the window, you would look up the hill road. On the crest, which was only just beyond our front door, the narrow road was guarded by pointed fir trees and a giant oak that overlooked the cricket meadow. You could not see further than this, because the ground fell gently away beyond it; but the road, of course, went on over the brow. On the left of it, as you walked down, was the Hollow, and the corner of the wonderful wood which maps call the Mount (but we called it Our Wood). On the other side was the cricket meadow, with its dozen dark oak trees, some of them sheltering the whitewashed shed which custom allowed us to call the Pavilion. In less than five minutes by this road

4

we are at the Chapel, and the meeting of three roads. The downward road leads to Marden and Maidstone, leagues away out of the world through the gap in the saucer. The upward road is home still.

If our hamlet were a village, and if the village had a street, this would be the street; for, although the cricket meadow and its trees are still on our right, all down the other side are houses: an alehouse with its own great cherry tree, a double cottage, then another double cottage where Dick Excell and his daughter live on one side and Groves and his daughter on the other—old Groves, himself like one of the figures of "Time" or the "Ancient of Days" in Blake's engravings, at this moment drawing water in buckets at the dipping-board of the cricket field pond. A little higher up, but still opposite the pond, is Jimmy's wood-working shed, whence came all the five-barred gates in fields and woods for miles around; then Jimmy's house on our left, on still rising ground, and the stable and barn and oast of the Farm on the right. Here, by its great thatched threshing barn, the road divided again; and if you took that branch which swept round the Farm to the right, and followed a short winding lane between a bank of fir trees and a nut plantation, you presently found yourself brought out upon the north and south road again, just under

5

the five ash trees at school. This was our shortest walk, and it was known as going round the Green.

But to see our northern boundaries it was necessary to bear to the left by the threshing barn, to swing up past Jimmy's house, past two cottages and "J. Baden, Universal Provider," a shop of all trades, and to pass even the cobbler's thatched hut, the last outpost of civilization, till you found yourself on a ten-foot road, with the edge of our hill—the hill of sand—close by the left-hand hedges.

Four miles ahead Staplehurst church stood up on the plain, and to the left the horizon hills were ten miles off, so that it was barely possible to distinguish houses or trees, because of their smallness. And at your feet, between these hills and you, lay a vast flat meadow-lightened plain, the Weald, capable of being silvered over in winter by long strips and stretches of flood.

On such a summer day as this the wide flats looked still and suffocating down there. Little winds came up among the honeysuckle and wild-rose hedges along the ridge of the hill; they stirred and sighed in the ten-acre cherry orchard behind you, where even now the noisy minder was beating tin pans and calling his bird-scaring halloo; but these winds missed the sunken flats of the Weald. There the sun burned down on green miles of hay and corn, and glittered hotly on the sleepy steamy woods, but nothing stirred there. Marden church with its pyramid-capped tower stood sultry and forsaken, only a thin streak of writhing smoke lay over the back of a toy train that threaded its way like a shuttle among poplars and willows four or five miles away, too far for a sound.

Far far away you could see the great gap in those hills where the Medway ran through at Yalding. Over the hills were Maidstone and the North Downs, visible on days of exceptionally clear atmosphere, and the mouth of the Thames, and London too; but these were all names on the lips of travellers, as far away from us as the Americas. Here was the gap in our great saucer where the strange and unimaginable world came flooding in over the Weald, over the Marden plains, and lapped at the foot of the hill on which we first touched earth. God might have run a gigantic finger softly round the rim of our credible world, starting west on the peak of Horseman-Den, brushing along all the soft horizon trees southwards to Brandfold and Gowdhurst, to the feather-edged Cranbrook woods, miles of them, from Hor-Den down to Staplehurst church, and then for more than a quarter of the circle above the tender blue shapes of hills unreal, never to be visited, and, passing over the place

7

where London was reputed to lie, would suddenly return to the firm rim of experience at the peak of Horseman-Den.

Thus the nursery, the school and its established gardens, made the base from which our unremembering souls sent forth inquiring sense and thought like worker bees, to gather in our knowledge of the world. There we began: we budded out of nothing, or came there, if we came, by ways of which no trace or memory remained; and every day our eyes looked under trees to where the sun got up and mounted high and sank again; every day we touched some leaf not touched by us before, finding everything created, ready, with a look of everlastingness when compared with the only standard we were born with, ourselves so new and changeable.

Swiftly and dangerously we generalized everything: we saw our neighbours' children as members of a permanent order, a kind of being existing side by side with beings of other kinds—men, for instance, and women, and uncles, and schoolboys—all stationary creatures to which our attitude was fixed for us by what seemed like long habit. Though we would now and then talk of growing-up, it was really a pretty piece of imagination and nothing more, and did not influence our present conduct of life for more than an hour. This world upon which our consciousness dawned, we dimly knew, must have been there before us; we came upon it when it was a going concern, dropped into pace with it, and, supposing that things had always been as we first found them (for the changes they underwent were too slow for our quick eyes), easily fell into the faith that they would always remain so. The only change we noted was an increase in our own powers over these permanencies, increase of physical strength or of power of persuasion or circumvention; but this only served to make them appear more fixed than ever.

2

The Wood

THERE is all the difference in the world between an object upon which your consciousness grows and one which grows upon your consciousness, and country-born people will all remember, with me, the shock of pain and doubt which comes when some well-known feature of a well-known land is suddenly removed—when a pond is drained, a barn demolished, or a tree cut up.

It is a law of copses, those dark close woods of bush-hazel and sapling chestnuts, that they shall be cleared every twelve years. The clearing of them provides the owner with thousands of chestnut bats, about four inches through at the bole and fourteen feet long, besides faggots and pea-boughs for himself and his cottagers. The chestnut bats will go as hop poles, tree-stilts, spiles, cordwood, hurdles and charcoal. A wood is a rich store of material; but it takes twelve years for the timber to grow to size from the stumps of the last cutting, though a wood that has been cleared becomes a wood again, to a child, in four years or even less.

Our wood was shaped like a fat letter L. It was

about four acres in extent; a little ditch-stream, but with plenty of rushes and willows, ran along it through what would be the horizontal stroke of the letter, and in the stem or vertical stroke was a sudden artificial mound, called the Mountain. I think it had been the dumping ground of waste earth and rubble from a pit in the next meadow where sand or sandstone had once been quarried, but now it was part of the wood, its steep sides were slippery with rich turkey moss, and it was all covered in with trees. The wood was near enough to the house as I measure distances to-day: only the garden, the long steep orchard, and the sandstone Hollow separated it from us, even on the darkest nights; but as we measured distance in those days it was far away, beyond a shout, beyond call therefore, and, folded down into the beginning of the valley there behind the bushy tops of a few hundred fruit trees, beyond sight too. For we did not measure distance by length but by remoteness, not by how far we had to go, or had come, but by how far away we felt, and a wood quickly shuts out the world. The wood fascinated us; yet it was not that we knew much about the world, or wished to be removed from it: it was not the call to exclude, but to enter, that we obeyed. A world there was, a nursemaid's place, whose laws unreasonably oppressed us sometimes; but though the wood

11

removed us from the petty reminders of those laws, it did not altogether shut them out. Down there, even among the ten million shielding leaves, a feeling of dinner-time could penetrate.

"You must have known," my mother would say. And I only shakily denied it, justifying a spiritual lie by a comma of material truth. The exact time I did not know; I had not, in truth, heard the bell; but you know when you are late, right enough, and the bare table was only a confirmation of my worst fears. What was I doing in the wood, then? It was impossible to tell, for to tell would make the golden time seem wasted; and I would stammer out my "Nothing," feeling indeed, now that I was no longer in the wood, that my condemnation was just. Fairy gold in the morning light is only dead leaves, they say; and this they say with sadness. But certainly it was gold once, yellow to see, and cold and satisfactory to handle: how can time or circumstance take away that goldenness? Joys we cannot lose, though any sorrow follows on their heels.

I did not go to the wood, then, to do anything, but to be there when things were happening. I had eaten my breakfast, and was mooning about the garden in that unhappy-happy state of nothing in particular to do, no uncommon state to be in at the third or fourth day of the summer holidays. There lay the whole long morning like a dusty avenue in front of me; I didn't want to hoe my garden, or to water it; besides, John had bagged the hoe. I walked about and idly wondered. I wondered if the grass in the Well field was nearly ready for cutting, if any apples showed signs of ripening, if the pigs were asleep—a score of idle wonders. In the mowing-grass of the Well field, looking for an apple which I had knocked down to taste, I found a bumble bee's nest, a matter for five minutes or ten. By the Hollow I threw an empty tin at an empty tin, and broke a low ash bough by hanging on it. There too I chased a cockerel a little, but let him get away because of the heat. And this brought me to the shallow end of the Hollow, where five slender ash trees shaded the entrance; and opposite me was the stile, and over the stile was the wood. I was there without intention, all alone there. The house and garden were buried, even on their hill top, by the boughs of many trees. There was no sound directly due to human beings, no shout, no voice at all, no fruit-pickers' call yet, no woodman's steady ham-hammer, no waggon rumbling. All the noises that I might have heard I heeded hardly at all. If sheep cried, or wind rustling fled down the valley, or flies buzzed, or bees hummed (and no doubt all these were audible), I accepted them all as part of the world, and they did not break the wall. There are times like these when solitude and silence mean the same thing. This solitude was a voice that I heard and could not refuse. Idle I was, by all useful standards, but I had already been alone a thousand times, and now I was alone by choice. It was no light and careless joy, however; there was an awe in it which easily turned to fear, and then I might have to take to my heels and run for company. Such idleness was a blessing. Long living in the country, long periods of being free and wild, had given us all as children the eyes of birds for quickness and a sharp ear for sudden sounds. These were the signs for which I looked and listened all about me; the hum and the greenness were constant and I overlooked them, they were the paper on which the verse was printed; but if a pheasant suddenly crowed or a red admiral settled on the hemlock stalks, I heard and saw and knew the signs at once.

I waited there, between the Hollow and the wood stile; you could not say that I hesitated, for to stand as near as I stood to the wood meant certainly to go in at last. But time had ended at the garden hedge, and there was no hurry. I looked, as you might say, at the handwriting, the stamp and the postmark of the wood, and then I climbed the stile and sat there on the flat nailed board, half in and half out of the hazel arbours—all the wood behind me, its seclusion at once a fear and an attraction, with the sunlit slope of the hayfield and orchard in front of me.

Presently, I put my other leg across the stile, and stepped down out of the sun into the dream. Each was as real as the other, but in entering the world of the wood, which has called itself a dream, though I was unconscious of any change in myself, I did indeed feel the lifting of authority. I went out of human nature, out of things native into things alien, out of the crowd of human influence into solitude. Things known are dismissed and done with, but things unknown, because of the possibilities they nourish, are at once desired and feared. I went, crossing the stile, from the world of the known to the world of the unknown, and walked on a tip-toe of spirit there. What had I been doing in the wood!

Leaves touched me; small as I was they swept my freckled face and red hair. I looked with a kind of breathless but friendly awe at the commonest sights—the yellow pimpernel, the bluebell seed-heads, the soft springy dry turkey mosses. I heard the leaves move, I heard the dry twigs snap, I heard my breath and my heart. I was always afraid in a wood, but not with an evil fear, unless sometimes I let it get the upper hand of me. Then fear seized me, and I would dash for the less confined parts of the wood. But all the time that I was this strange half-frightened creature I was a boy as well, peering and prying, excitedly interested in the details of the wood, dipping my shoe in the red rusty mud, cutting and peeling a stick to poke in holes and buries, a creature of the senses of touch and sight and smell, harvesting by leaf and seed and snail-shell, with meticulous notice of every detail, the substance of this teeming world into which I had been so surprisingly born.

The whole of the wood was one creature, and that one spoke somehow to my spirit; but the wood was also a multitude of creatures, and these spoke, less strangely, to my eager senses. I picked strange flowers and dropped them soon for others, and these I dropped again readily enough when, down in the reedy parts, I found wild raspberries ripe. I searched for old nests, for hidden rabbits, for moorhens: I dashed myself through brambles for a moth, I proudly drew down hazel branches for their green nuts. They were soft as yet, full of sour white pith, but with a tiny tender kernel, no meal for the smallest mouse. Yet I ate them, and what made them sweet was my pride that I had found them for myself. I saw weird stagshorn fungi branching out of the spongy ground, and bright orange jellies on dead twigs in dark places, and shelves of the beefsteak fungus jutting out from the boles of dead or dying trees.

After a time the guilty feeling of lateness began to weigh me down. I had refused to entertain a conscience, but it would not be denied. The disobedience became flagrant, extremely dark and uncomfortable. I knew why Adam hid; I knew he didn't believe that his excuses would even sound plausible; and at last, when the voice wouldn't be silenced and the wood itself began to refuse to connive at my lateness, I twisted and dodged my way quickly to the stile, and then hurried through the field as though a minute saved might really put the clock back; and arrived quite as late as I had expected.

Space, perhaps, is the picture of Time, and as unreal. It is a relation between entities of matter, just as time is a relation between events: near and far, long and short, will tell us of Time or Space. There is no real moment in eternity, no position in infinity. With that image of the saucer I tried to make our world seem small and finite by contrast with the vastness beyond it. But on the circumference of infinity, at the point where, being born, we feel our feet, we can explore in two directions —for that is the nature of infinity: that you are never nearer the beginning than the end. If you see yourself standing on a circle, facing the unknowable centre, you can walk to the right or left, indifferently. The only necessity, since you live, is to go on. With us there was no opportunity to go on over the rim of that twenty-mile saucer—we had to go into the wood (as one might say) and find detail upon detail, tree in wood, branch on tree, leaf on branch, vein on leaf, sap in vein: and this minuteness in a million common things—and that was infinity too. The smallness of our world could not shut us out of the world's immensity. Deeper we looked and learned, till that habit became our nature, and now we cannot violate it.

As for the wood, autumn followed summer, the nuts ripened and we gathered them, then the acorns, and then the chestnuts, and we shook the trunks and pricked our fingers with the husks and filled our pockets with chestnuts. Then the leaves, already turning, grew gold, grew brown, fell down and rusted and rotted, and the mud came and the cold and frost of winter. In winter, naturally, we did not often go to the wood. One day, however, we overheard our father talking about Jack Strawberry, a woodman, and gathered that Our Wood was being cut down. John and I slipped away as soon as we could, to see this for ourselves, expecting only delight. But as we turned the corner by the Hollow the sight of the change hurt our inexperienced hearts. In spite of the thrill of a new world revealed by the clearing, something unhappy and maleficent was in the air. I knew nothing of death then, but I remember the feeling of dismay, and now I know that it was the same: that what has been will never be again, that the wood, which was a symbol, a living creature, almost a person to us, was going out of existence. It was not that we felt any sentimental sorrow for the trees that were down or were crashing; the hurt was not made in the world, but in us. If this wood, which had stood there in all our interminable lives, could so be destroyed, what might not go? And in that first sight of the empty place we became aware, though never so faintly, of our own insecurity. It was nothing really; in a week we had, like sensible children, accepted the new wood, with its tree stumps, its piles of bats and faggots; and we soon played happily over the very ruins of the wood we had lost. Besides, how good the destruction was for the primroses. In a spring or two, when the new suckers had shot up again out of the old stumps, it was possible to treat the place as a wood again; and then the old wood came back, changed in details, but in presence exactly the same. I was seven or eight years old then; but the feeling of loss was so strong while it lasted, that although the later clearings could not, of course, hurt in the same way, they never failed to revive in me the memory of that sudden empty perplexity.

3

My Mother's Mother

M Y mother's mother had suffered ill-fortune all her life. She was a Waddington, daughter of a wealthy leather merchant. She often told us that when she was a girl she had everything she wanted at the mere wish. She loved to be drawn into memories, to let us know what a flirt she could be, to tell us, in 1919, of how she once smoked a cigar, what balls she attended, what songs and duets she sang and played, what arts she used in order to get a favour from her father—whom she called Pa or Papa, in the fine novelist's manner. Pa, however, in spite of his fondness for his little Jenny, seems to have been a brute. He drank a great deal of rum; and took a great fancy to one of his grandchildren, now my mother, who confesses with what terror she would hear him call her to play cribbage with him, and how furiously he would rage over his rum if he lost the game. "And often and often," my mother says, "I have cheated, so that he should win." Yet this old man was generous in a business-like way, and when my grandmother was first married he

calmly offered her five pounds for every confine-
ment—a preposterous offer which he kept to the
letter.

My mother's father, grandfather to us children in
no more than name, for he died a year after my
mother's marriage, was an engraver and die-sinker,
a very jolly light-hearted and worldly fellow. He
must have been good company, and a good craftsman, but a poor hand at business. All that I remember of him is an enlarged photograph—he wore
whiskers—and a collection of copper plates, dies,
designs and engraver's tools which my grandmother
gave me when I was too young to know that one day
I should be sorry not to have kept them.

Their engagement was announced when my
grandmother was a girl of eighteen, and to me has
descended what must have been a tiny occasion of
great delight between them. It is her photograph,
on glass, as she would always proudly add, because
this being on glass, it seems, was the newest wonder
in photographs; but how much more a personal
possession it is than the large artistic portraits of
to-day. I must go and fetch it, that I may have it
before me while I tell about it, for a whole vanished
human age perfumes it. She was eighteen, I say,
and betrothed, and it was soon to be John's first
engaged birthday. Photography was still a wonder,

21

silhouettes were going out of fashion, miniatures were common; they lived in London; this present must be unique and a surprise. The cost is no difficulty; papa has been consulted, and he was jocular and pleasant about it. Jenny is proud of her dress too, her gold necklet and her hair. So the appointment is made, the carriage called, and in the strangeness of evening dress in daylight, Jenny drives off to the photographer's studio, is posed, screwed into position, and the exposure is made. The photographer is all grace and patience. In what style will she have it mounted? She looks at the examples he shows her and chooses this: a small red morocco folding case, velvet lined, to open like a book; the photograph, delicately coloured, mounted inside in a gold filigree frame with an oval opening. Madam shall have it in ten days, if that will do.

"I must," says my grandmother, "oh, I must have it before the 22nd." The photographer notes her blushes, smooths his black whiskers, smiles understandingly, and promises it for the 20th.

It was hard to say nothing to Little John, as papa called him. Lucky for Little John that pa liked him, for pa was a bluff and boisterous fellow, and would have broken the match if he had not blessed it. But if Jenny felt guilty about keeping a secret, she kept it, nevertheless. On the 20th the photographer's man in uniform called, and the maid brought Miss Jenny a sealed parcel. Jenny opened it in the safe silence of her room. Rolled in tissue paper was the red morocco folding case. She looked at her ring, and at the photograph. A dozen times that day the tissue paper was unfolded again, the little catch loosened, and the photograph compared with the face in the mirror; and when the 22nd came at last, Jenny (who knows by what plausible devices?) has managed to steal into John's room and put the portrait under his pillow.

They were both young and therefore deep in the idyll of love, and now because they are dead the red morocco case lined with velvet is mine. I speak to my grandmother now when she is only eighteen, and know what kind of a girl she is. She has a calm and humorous spirit. There is the beginning of a smile on her mouth, and a grand look of certainty in affection in her direct eyes. Here she sits quietly; her left arm rests on a covered table, the hand hanging down to show the ring, which the photographer, good fellow, has made clearer with a touch of his gold. Her right hand plays lightly with the long gold necklace, so long indeed that her hand rests among the silks of her flounced dress. She has gold earrings, too, and a round locket brooch at her throat, in which locket, small as it is, the collar and

23

whiskers of Little John can be made out. She was always proud of her hair, which was a dark glinting brown, and here it is carefully dressed by her woman, looped down over the ears and coiled in a great plait over the top of her head. She is not pretty: her mouth is too big, too kind: but her eyes are deep enough, and though the fun is not lighting them now, because her lover is not there, there is about her the beauty of a fine youthful spirit in repose.

She was happy enough then, but her victory was that she was still happy at seventy, when, but for the old age pension, she had nothing saved out of the years between. Either John was unpractical, a craftsman and not a man of business, or unfortunate, or extravagant; and all her father's fortune, though his gifts saved them often while he lived, was lavished on a third wife, Ruth, the designing house-keeper. On no less than twelve occasions my grand-mother was confined, as they said; and true to his promise the old man sent his five pounds every time. But of all those babies only four grew up.

Her life was a long struggle with illness and poverty and, I suppose, disappointment, of which, when she was old, she never chose to speak much. She would rather tell me about the flourishing en-graver's business, the details of the craft; how Jack used to sit down with pencil and paper of an evening and design the most delicate ingenious monograms, which he would cut on a die the following week and print and present to his relations on their birthdays. She would tell how busy he was, and how playful; how they lived, I think, under the workshops, where the engraving and embossing was done, and how sometimes she would climb up to the top room to see the girls at work on the presses. Then her hands would move to show how dies were inked and cleaned with a wipe of the hand, how they were put in the press, and the heavy lever of the screw was spun for printing; and while she spoke her eyes were glad to be back in the dingy parts of London, discounting now the heavy chestnut woods that waved outside her windows, and the geraniums and cyclamens of which she was usually so proud. She would not speak of sorrows sadly—not at all unless your questions made her do so—but most willingly and most vividly of her girlhood, and she seemed to find comfort now, when she was poor, in recalling how spoilt she once had been by her rich papa.

She lived, too, among her own pieces of history: pictures, ornaments, furniture, enough to furnish her two small rooms, all breathed tales to her, and the greatest source of inspired reminiscence was a thick-leaved photograph album, bound and clasped in brass, whose heavy leaves turned over like lids, slowly, while she related histories, any one of which was all that there is in a novel.

My first recollection of this grandmother is also one of the earliest of my life. For some reason unknown to me, some force of a cruel world whose cruelty did not touch a baby of four, she came down to our part of the country, and was installed for a time in the lonely farm-house of Hor-Den, which belonged to my other grandfather, the schoolmaster. It still stands, though strangely altered by the cutting down of the trees and the cobnut plantation and privet hedges, which walled it in when I lived there in a kind of paradise. I was only four. The cowshed was a vast dark cave to me, the big hay barn a place to get lost in, so that I did not stray to the farm buildings much unless she, or the old cowman, took me there and held my hand. But the lawn, beautifully overgrown and neglected, the lawn shaded by apple trees and a walnut tree, and sheltered on its four sides: on the north by the walls of barn and cowshed, on the west by these fruit trees and a dense nut plantation, on the south by a quick-and-privet hedge on a bank and an orchard beyond it, and on the east by a tall hedge of laurels and laburnum and the house itself—this lawn was a wilderness of joy to me, and it was full of grasshoppers. Here I would play all day, with granny running to look out at me (for I was a treasure then) from time to time. I do not remember what I did there: I had a box of tools I think, the first of many; and sometimes I would go ever so far away from the house, quite to the other side of the lawn, in a brave fear, and listen to the lowings of the cows when they came up through the mud at milking time, and the echoing clatter of pails and churns inside, and the whirring ghostly noise of that separator in the clean brick-paved dairy at Mrs Excell's.

The farm-house of Hor-Den was a white stucco and boarded structure, with square sash windows on each side of the porch, and a lean-to conservatory or vine-house on the left, opening out of the kitchen. It was very dark indoors where a wainscoted passage ran straight down the middle of the house from the front door to the stairs, between the rooms. At the far end, where the stairs went up to the right, was a door which was never opened, at least in my sight.

A door that is never seen open is always something of a mystery; but this door, I had been answered, if opened would lead at a step into Mrs Excell's kitchen. It still seems romantic to me. I was, I felt, one of Harry Excell's greatest friends.

He was the tall, loose-limbed, grizzled cowman who sometimes took me into the cowshed with him. He had a personal fashion in whiskers, for he shaved his throat and the round point of his chin once a week, and had all the complement of manliness except a beard. This made his face square and homely. His eyes were as blue as speedwell flowers, with small, sharp pupils. Because his natural habit of mind was kindly, the wrinkles of his eyes and brow were kindly too—for face wrinkles are nothing but habits of expression, some of thought, some of scorn, some of hardness of heart, some of weakness, gentleness, laughter or perplexity. Harry's were the tale of ready smiling and true country gentleness to children. He always spoke to me as friend to friend, without any of the false humour or lack of seriousness which less understanding grown-ups use towards children. I liked him: he wasn't afraid of cows as I was. There was one brown and white cow in particular whom I feared. She was called the "Great Fat Kicker," and it was necessary to bind her tightly with a band of hard rope about her girths before she would stand to be milked. Harry showed no fear of her or any animal, and I should have stood in loving awe of him for this, if for no other reason. It was not because I realized that *he* lived on the other side of the unopenable door that it filled me

28

with a pleasant kind of terror. The noises that came to me through its panels did not include his soft bass. They were noises of a fury of cleanliness— washing, washing-up, sweeping and hurrying to and fro, and sometimes, I think, of loud and angry voices, one of which was Harry's voice, no doubt, but not the voice I knew.

Children have no reasons for antipathies and affections. I did not merely passively dislike Mrs Excell, I flew from her in terror, as I would always fly from strange and unknown manifestations. There was never any geniality about her; and when I saw her dark, drawn face look out of the scullery window, or her blue print dress flutter in the dairy or in the yard, real terror assailed my four-year-old heart, and I would run to granny, not so much to be out of the way of the old dairywoman as to be in the refuge of good company; for I never told my fears, but rather disguised them, lest they should become known to Mrs Excell. And I see now that my instincts were right, for her fury against dirt and disorder was an expression of a desire for mastery: she was a frus- trated woman, with no children of her own, and if she had known how her voice or glance had power for terror over me, she would certainly have found exquisite pleasure in using them for small but subtle cruelties. Later on, when I came to read of witches, my mental picture of them all was based on the disturbing presence and personality of Mrs Excell. Because of her the door at the end of the dark passage had a sinister look, and I was glad it was never opened.

Much later in my life, when my grandfather was dead, Harry came to work as gardener, pigman and general odd-job man about the school, and then these very early associations were revived, but by that time my brother John had supplanted me and become his favourite. We boys were a plague to him too, borrowing his hatchets and billhooks for our private woodcraft, and never, I'm afraid, remembering to return them unasked. Still, all Harry's cunning, even then, would only lead him to hide his tools in simple places, and if we could not find them he would, for a promise, always tell us where.

Moving from Hor-Den meant, for him, moving into a small half cottage—that one with its own cherry tree standing opposite the pond in the cricket meadow. There, quite suddenly, his witch-wife surrendered in the war she had waged so long and so furiously against dirt, and Harry found himself living with a woman who, forfeiting a wide reputation for spotless housewifery, became a byword and a warning in the place. But he didn't complain to us. He had, as I said, a pleasant voice and a kind

30

chuckle-laugh, rather childlike; I never saw him unkind or cruel, yet I heard that at this time he sometimes beat his wife. Her eyes became wilder, her mutterings more incoherent; she was to the village children that kind of terror which one dares to shout at and laugh at in company, but only to laugh and run away; and if a child of this sort met her alone he would silently pass as fast as not running permitted, as wide as the road away, and look back often till she was gone. She was morose, friendless, thin, ragged, in these later years, and no gossip.

Harry died of gangrene of the foot, perhaps of dirt and neglect. But he was old then, and knew that he wouldn't work any more. To a countryman, the prospect of not working is the prospect of dying. My father went in often to see him; he would inquire after John, perhaps; but as for the rest, a world where you could not work was a world to leave. He suffered the pain and inaction patiently a little while, but shook his head one day to my father's attempt to cheer him, and said, "No, no. I reckon I be prit'nigh beazled out," and next day he died. After his death Mrs Excell was taken away to the infirmary. She was mad, or at any rate too mad to be allowed to live alone.

I stopped for a digression from those happy days with my grandmother at Hor-Den because the existence of Mrs Excell there was one of the facts which loom large now in the tiny memories remaining; though perhaps the rather terrified and mysterious regard I had for her for the rest of my life had its real beginning in the strange influence on my imagination of a door that never opened.

I have not entered the house for nearly thirty years, so that no clear and continuous picture remains. I have, for example, no recollection of the shape and look of the kitchen, except, as I say, of this dark end of the passage, where the kitchen was reached by turning to the left and the staircase by turning to the right; nor, indeed, a clear picture of any of the rooms but two: the bedroom where I slept with my grandmother, and the room immediately underneath, the first right-hand door of the wainscoted passage, the room where we took our breakfast at a round table—just the two of us—and where I learned with surprise that all people do not eat milk and porridge in the same way. For granny taught me to dig a small pond, I called it, in the middle of my porridge, and to pour my cold milk into that. It was not the family way at home; there we let the milk fill the edges of the plate and mount, to some extent, the rounded plateau. But if granny's method was revolutionary, it was all the more exciting to try. I was not old enough to see the science in such a method, although I knew (who does not?) by painful experience that the middle parts of a plate of porridge remained hot too long. While I stayed with granny I did as granny did, and with new delight every morning; but I returned to family methods when I came home again, and did not change until, in due time, I was allowed to refuse porridge altogether. Its stodgy sweet nature had always revolted me, unless it was burnt, when I thought it had a flavour worth tasting.

I slept upstairs at Hor-Den on one side of a double-bed, not the side where the small table stood with its books and its glass of water. Granny, of course, put me to bed, though she taught me something of how to undo and do up buttons. It was a high feather-bed, and I had to be lifted into it; but when I had said my prayers, and before I was lifted to bed, she would take an apple, all polished, out of the pocket of her black and shiny dress, show it to me, and then put it up on a shelf of the overmantel beside the little silver milk churn, where it would stay till morning. In the morning it would be mine to eat in bed while granny dressed. But now—the soft, high, white, cool bed, the sinking into the belly of the pillow, the safe pinioning of hands by the strait-waistcoat of the turn-back of sheets and blankets, the sweet and virtuous influence of white linen upon a tired little boy, who was, after this comforting ritual, ready enough to be kissed good-night and to promise to be good—the only likeness of wickedness being to call out or cry in the deeps of the bed, granny having gone downstairs again to sew by lamplight—this, or something very like this, is many a man's clean and early recollection, and it is not because of these memories that men find any comfort in the promise of a heaven of which, to recommend it, a visionary said: There shall be no night there. No, this gentle gradual fall of night and sleep, after such an infancy, is a pure blessing of God.

The day had hardly retired before me in those days. Grandmother drew the curtains to shut out the end of twilight, but left a lamp in its iron standing-stove on the floor. It was there for warmth, but it gave me light; and with this chance light, quite unregarded by my granny, I played myself into dreams. For the lamp cast a wavering wheel of light upwards upon the white ceiling, and I would lie back into the pillow, soothed by the certain promise of that apple on its shelf beside the silver churn, and let the swimming circles of light and shadow make pictures there for my delight.

A snowy scene, with children running, and sudden falls of fallen snow from pine-tree branches waving in the wind, and a long road with no grass edges now, because the settled snow covers all from hedge to hedge in white—I remember this so well that I can see it all again. It was not a picture to hang on the wall or to find in a book; indeed, it was not an experience of the eyes at all, though it came in that way, but the eddying rhythm of a snowy day, and the cries, and the glowing coldness: the soul of a lovely experience agitating with delight the soul of a little boy falling asleep. I know so many things now that I knew nothing of then: this slight, quick, almost feverish restlessness of the light and shadow were produced, I suppose, by the swirling up-currents of hot air from the lamp; the wheel-shape was only the gigantic indistinct shadow of the perforated top of the iron stove, and the pictures and the magic were all in my head. But I was not puzzled about the shape or a reason for its move-ment then, and I only wished that my grandmother would come in unexpectedly, to see the snow scenes so real upon her ceiling. The pictures fluctuated and changed with all the acceptable inconsistency of dreams; and I lay there and watched them changing, fascinated by a performance I never dreamed was my own, until I was neither awake nor asleep, until I was asleep.

And then, you remember, it was morning; day was apparent even through the curtains, grand-mother was asleep beside me, and my whole desire was for the apple by the silver churn. Every morning I woke granny to give me the apple, and as I ate it I dearly coveted the little silver churn. Milk churns were familiar to me from my visits to the cowshed, but they were so tall, in those days, that I had to be lifted to look inside. Inside, indeed, there was almost room for me. I could not move one, even if it was empty, and yet, when they were full of milk, Harry could tip them lightly on to their wheel-rim, and with his hand on the hub of the lid he trundled them easily over the noisy stone floor to the cart, where two men lifted them up and, when the cart was loaded, drove them away to the station. But on the overmantel shelf in grandmother's bedroom, on the shelf which held my morning apples, stood a perfect miniature model of a churn. And I coveted this, and repeatedly asked if I might have it. To my mind it was the perfect toy; to granny's mind, however, it was an ornament, a treasure, and not for children. "When I grow up to be a man, granny," I said, "I shall take you out for walks with me." But I might not have the churn now, only sometimes to look at and into for a moment. "You shall have it," said my grandmother, "for your very own, when you grow up to be a man." Alas, I never saw it again, for soon afterwards granny went away, and, as for me, I returned to the war and peace of family life.

36

4

The Night Nursery

MEMORIES of very early days are strangely detached. Though we may be at any moment the sum of all our experiences, many experiences which must have been important in their influences upon our later lives have been quite forgotten, and what suddenly flashes into mind is something bright but trivial, with no place in the story of our lives to account for its survival. These memories are neither striking nor significant, they are like little detached pieces of a jig-saw puzzle; but they are intensely pleasant, because they are tiny footholds on a vague wide-extending country of the past. We remember them without any attempt: the will has nothing to do, the mind lies like a quiet well; when one of these memories will rise like a bubble, and within the limits of a lost moment will make us children again.

I am quiet, thinking of nothing; I see the kitchen garden again, hot and dry in the summer sun, with plantain leaves lying outstretched on the yellow dusty clay, and grass blades, and little stray sticks from the faggots in the wood-lodge. The wood-lodge is near; it is built of great slabs of wood from Jimmy's timber-yard, slabs flat inside, but rounded outside: the first few of the strips cut when a whole natural tree is laid on the saw bench. The door is open, the shed is dark, I can smell the acid smell of dead wood; the handbill is struck on the tripod chopping block inside, it bites into the scarred head of the tripod. Behind me is the warm brick wall of the school, like a windowed cliff. Over my head are cherry-tree branches, but without any cherries; and I am with Winnie, our first nurse. I do not remember how we came to be there, nor where we went from there. My brain, for some unexplained reason, snapshotted that bright red and green moment and this afternoon gave it back to me. Winnie holds in her hand, for me to see it, a cast glass jubilee mug, with the picture of Queen Victoria embossed upon it in a circle, and the rest of the mug all rough with crusted wreaths and frost-like glass. The school behind is unusually empty, everyone else has gone away to a picnic. Bit by bit I could recover every colour and detail of the picture, and I know that I remember all the world at that instant because of the Jubilee Mug.

Or again, it is afternoon, that do-nothing time of the day before tea, and I am waiting by the big bed in my mother's room. I wear my pinafore. I have nothing to do. I cannot remember if my mother is there dressing or not. I only see a small brown picture on the wall over my cot, a picture of a little boy with a crust of bread in his hand screaming because he is surrounded by four or five long-necked geese. I only see the brass rings and knobs at the foot of my mother's bedstead, and find that my fingers *will* turn them, unscrewing the little golden balls, a thing forbidden to children, and making the elaborate metal framework all loose and rattling.

All around such memories as these is a grey sea of nonentity; no time past or to come, no progress of events is recalled, but a very definite state of mind and mood of the world; the total of all feelings, characterized by summer sun and dust out of doors, or afternoonishness, or some other unnameable completeness; so that if I could only find the word, one word would completely express the memory. For though these child-pictures are fragmentary in the sense that they don't fit into any philosophy of experience, they are characteristically complete to the person remembering them. As soon as action comes in they become a different kind of memory altogether. I can recall the mixed warmth and cold of Christmas morning, when we children would wake before daylight to scramble out of bed for our filled stockings; but as soon as I begin to remember the actions and the conversations across the ghostly

39

dark, I know I am not recalling an occasion, but a sketchy kind of knowledge of several occasions: not what we did then, but what we used to do. Then all the vivid and unreasonable colours go out; I think of those Christmas mornings, but I do not see them, or if I do, I see them by creating, and not because they are so startlingly clear. What I do see and remember is the frost, ferned upon window-panes through which the grey light of day is beginning to shine; and an untidy bed, now only warm in places; and feet coldly thrust out from flannel nightgowns, and the stiff starchiness, the dutiful cold cleanness of linen now to be put on for Christmas Day, which begins like a monstrous big Sunday.

Another of those vivid and very early impressions of a complete moment photographed upon the memory comes into my head often with lamplight. I am in a blanket and in somebody's arms. The house is a sub-nocturnal cave, the air close and flavoured with food, the room lit by the brown light of a big lamp in the middle of the table, and the flickering of a well-established fire in the grate. People are at supper, all looking up unfamiliarly in the lamplight as I am carried in. My mother is there, but without her children; a great and noisy company of grown-ups fills the children's places: Mr Plumbridge, the young schoolmaster, is in Carrie's place, Miss

Richardson in mine, Miss Collins in Stella's, and many others whom I had never thought of as eaters at all, a roomful of feasting usurpers it seems to me, awake, when Time is dead, in that part of night that is not temporal at all, between two sleeps, as unreal as a dream itself. Very like a dream, indeed; for all dreams have this black enclosing background, this confined light, and this strangeness made of familiar places and people, fantastically altered and doing unexpected things with ease. Supper was a legendary meal, which was not laid when I left for bed and was generally all cleared away long before I was up.

What I think must be a feeling shared by many, is the strong impression left in my mind of houses by artificial light—a sense, to express it so, of ceilings and walls and black windows and all the unreality of imprisonment. Not that the house seemed smaller by artificial light—it seemed indeed much larger—but it was cavernous, and, though I could not have defined it so, a hopeless refuge from the nothing of night. Doors and windows in particular changed their natures. The outside world by winter night was not a world of our experience at all, so that we could not let our imagination go out by them. These nights annihilated our world; we did not think about the trees in darkness, nor the stars among their branches, nor the dim grey lines of lanes, because we had not as yet seen them. For a long time the fall of dark was either a signal for bed, or an event that happened while we were in bed. Just as we thought that dinner-time was a naturally ordained mid-day pause, and never troubled about the human effort maintaining it, so we thought the fall of night and going to bed was only the natural end of the day and time. Anyhow, one of the most vivid and mysterious of childish memories, one which, indeed, never quite loses its romantic power, is a lamplit tea-time, when the short winter day dies before bed-time, before the day's work and play can properly be called ended; and a meal, planned as a daylight meal, has to be taken by night. This is the time of celery and chrysanthemums, or of plates built high with hot slices of dark, buttered toast, the time of the beginning of fires, and the first sign of a complete change of the programme of life, which must now be played for the most part indoors.

It was our mother's rule that children went to bed early. We children were washed nightly in a brown bath shaped rather like an armchair; it had a high, sloping back, and two handles where the arms of a chair would have been. I thought that these handles were ledges for flannel and soap, and unsuccessful experiments to use them for these failed to convince me that the idea was wrong. I only thought the ledges ill-constructed. Perhaps they were handles to hold when emptying the bath, or hand-grips by which to pull oneself out of the bath. But my mother always pulled us out, and always too soon. There was, however, a reward for the good, a special treat—it was a warmed towel. I have never tried it since, but the comforting memory remains and the sweet, warm toasting smell. Your body, roughly dried, was suddenly smothered in a white and odorous softness—the precise moment had to be watched, it would never do to spoil a warmed towel with too wet a skin, so you dried yourself, standing on the bath-mat while nursery firelight flickered on the other towel hung over the tall wire guard. Then your mother snatched the hot towel quickly off the guard, and enveloped you as you stood. The final drying, fingers, toes, ears and hair (oh, that hair rubbing!), was done for you while you sat in the towel on her knees. Then came a nightgown over your head and down to your feet, and prayers, and a cot with shiny cold iron bars and four brass knobs like four dutch doll's heads in gold.

We did not say our prayers in the morning—(a custom followed by children in books sometimes, and one which we thought very strange)—but at night. Prayers increased in number according to ages, and had no titles except the first two or three words of the prayer. Each child named himself in the family list, impersonally and in proper place and by his own christian name—and thus this prayer, the "Pray God Bless," was a standard form. When another baby was born we added him on at the end of the list, and called him baby until the name was fixed. Everyone said this prayer; but as we grew older we learned more: "Gentle Jesus," and "Our Father." "Gentle Jesus" was really the verse of a hymn and we sometimes sang it with our mother instead of saying it. It was often left to us to say our prayers "to ourselves" as we called it. Small children, of course, said them aloud; but with the others races in prayers were frequently held when we said them in silence. The winner, however, had to answer to the recognized list afterwards, and if it was found that he had omitted any, out of bed and down on his knees he had to go again. It was despicable to say prayers in bed, and was only forgiven on very cold nights. Not uncommonly we forgot to say our prayers until sleepiness reminded us. "Oh," said someone, "I didn't say my prayers! Did you?" Company makes courage easier, and generally if one had forgotten so had another, and out we both would get.

Bed is the throne of the kingdom of fancy and fear. We did not like the enforced change from the other kingdom: no more than other children were we ever ready to go to bed. The bath by the nursery firelight is far more attractive in memory than it ever was in immediate prospect. Children always resent changes forced upon them by laws of time, because the necessity of laws is not plain to them; and the call to bed always meant an unexpected end to games which we had been playing as though they were endless. The bath was nothing better than a consolation, and till we were in bed, bed was not even that. But we made the best of it. We had many games to play in the dark; speaking games, in which one posed the questions and the others guessed. Children also love to play with words and change the sounds about, and as there are many interchangeable sounds, this was a game, a queer game indeed, which we often employed to pass the dark pleasantly. But very young children soon go to sleep.

When my younger brother and I, aged about five and seven, were promoted to a room of our own, one of our amusements was to work together in a tale. One tale went on night after night, and really consisted of a number of adventures joined together only by the name of the hero. We called him Meri-winkle, and he was always having the most astonishing desirable presents given to him. Once he had the works of a clock given to him by his father. Magic was one of his accomplishments; he could fly and blow down great trees. Nominally we were to take it in turns to invent some new adventure for him, but my brother had a queer habit of falling asleep on the spur of the moment. He would finish a sentence, and quiet would reign, but he had not finished the tale. I used to call to him and get no reply; and often, when it had been my turn to tell the story, I would go proudly on with the hero and give him the usual climax to his adventure, only to find at last that John had been asleep for the best work.

Dreams at that age I cannot now recall, though I think we did dream, and in the morning often told our dreams to each other. I can remember dreaming that a hand came to my pillow holding out to me a plate full of bread and butter. I smelt that smell and reached out a hand to take a slice. What astonished me, so that I still remember it, was that one should be so deceived as to reach out a real hand (and so wake up) for what was so obviously a dream plate. I can also remember both of us falling out of bed. But if I do not remember many dreams, I well remember the delicious panorama on the dark, which slowly unrolled before me while I was falling asleep. Faces, flowers, lovely fern-like leaves, trees, and fruit, and slowly moving animals (I think all in miniature, and certainly all in dim colours on a velvet black background) went slowly floating down before me from ceiling to floor, just beyond the foot of the bed. And I was so conscious of enjoying this time of delight that I not only looked forward to it (John being asleep long ago) but made great efforts to prolong it, for I used to believe that if I only tried hard enough the lovely panorama would roll back from floor to ceiling and give me all those passing fancies again. The very effort, I suppose, sent me to sleep. But certainly such delightful visions were partly under control, and they lasted with me till I was fifteen or sixteen.

These unreal sights were never horrible or terrifying, but real sounds and unexplainable sights used to frighten me. I was a little ashamed of my fears too, and would often endure them for an hour rather than call out to my brother, who was two years my junior and sound asleep on the other side. One night the tales had finished in that disappointing way. I think I had dozed a little, then suddenly I was wide awake. A loud and terrible sound came from the passage: moans and long sighs of suffering beginning to come nearer and nearer. To our wall, which was only a thin partition of wood, they drew near; it was an agony. They passed by and died down slowly into a silence that was menacing and horrible. I woke John by shaking him, and asked him what it was. By the time that he was awake no sound was left. He had heard nothing; he sleepily made reply that he didn't know, and turned back into sleep. I have never known what that noise was, and I shall never find out. But I am writing this now late at night in the same house. John is married and lives on an island far away. Everyone else in the house is in bed. I know it is a quiet and harmless starry night, yet the effort of recalling that terrifying noise has made my heart go cold again.

5

The Front Hall Cupboard

BECAUSE we lived at a school, our home, like the stage house, had no fourth wall. If you entered by the front door, at once the chilly formality of politeness to visitors met you; there you stood on the big blue and yellow tiles of the tiny square hall, with the door shut behind you, the key in the lock all day, the iron letter-box slot in the door too, a single pane of glass let deep into the bricks on right and left of the hall, and in front of you folding doors with little panels of engraved glass. On the sill, or on the umbrella stand, lay a large red-edged hymn book, for Aunt Mary's use on Sundays; and, indeed, the Sunday feeling hung about in this dampish little box all through the week: one was never at home in the hall. On the other side of the glass door and partition things were hardly more cheerful. The drawing-room door on the left had porcelain knobs and finger-plates, white with gold outlines, cold to the touch; and on the right, surprising you with their nearness to the hall and the world outside, the front stairs began with a cramped right-angled sweep. Straight ahead, even on sunny days, was a long passage of dark, and a cupboard under the stairs full of the queerest lumber: packets of new boot-brushes, scrubbing-brushes, bootlaces, rolls of wallpaper, and a medley of cardboard boxes and string and crumpled sheets of stiff brown paper. Whoever was lucky enough to receive a parcel had to untie the string and not cut it, had to fold the brown paper neatly, preserve the cardboard box and put it all in its proper place—the hall cupboard. It was my firm though vague belief that some unmentionable and fabulous Thing lived in this cupboard. Not a real Thing, you must understand, who would do anything so definite as to attack or eat you, nothing that you could be sure you had seen or heard, certainly nothing to describe, nothing to fear for what it might do, but a formless terror, just as fearful to think of safely shut in behind the door as if it were moving abroad and breathing the chill and sunless air of the hall and passage. Moreover the Presence polluted all this end of the house, and it required resolution to go there alone. Long after-wards, quite nonchalant and grown up, I spoke of this fear to my eldest sister, and each was surprised that the other knew it. It infected the drawing-room, whose door would not latch, but had to be locked and the key left in the keyhole; its presence could be felt like a vapour as you descended the front stairs; and nowadays (unless it was indeed some evil memory belonging to the house) I think I know what it was. The haunted parts of the house were the sunless parts. The front door opened north, and no sun ever came into that tiled well of a hall. The drawing-room windows looked north and east, but tall trees, hedges and a grass bank across the road prevented the little morning sunlight that might have got in that way. There were no other windows in that part of the house, except a window on the landing at the top of the stairs, a west window; and the fear did not begin till, in your progress to the hall, that window was passed; and just beyond the cupboard a kind of midget conservatory which only caught the last rays of summer light, and the fear did not quite extend to this. The drawing-room was of all places perhaps the least cheerful, for it was never used except as a receiving-room into which visitors were shut while the person they wanted was fetched from the live and echoing building beyond. On Sundays, in the winter, it is true, the family sat by the drawing-room fire, or stood round the American Organ to sing, before we children were sent to bed. Peopled like this with a fire and a song the place was quite transformed, but in the ordinary days of the week this end of the house was not an inhabited place at all, it was right out of the proper kingdom even of ubiquitous children, and it frightened us by its cold reserves.

To leave this unfriendly piece of the outside world shut into our home by mistake, there were two ways: the stairs, or the doorway opposite the cupboard of mystery. By either way one entered upon more dark and narrow passages, and dark unexpected steps down, of which strange visitors had to have timely warning. Upstairs there were three steps down suddenly from the landing, and the passage led to the precipice of the backstairs and the door of the nursery. Downstairs, opposite the cupboard in the hall, was a door above one step, a door never shut. Here at bright noon a solemn darkness reigned. Over the door-head hung the bell on a curly spring which, by means of wires and levers, was ingeniously connected to the bell-pull at the front door. One vigorous pull by the postman set this bell quivering, almost angrily, on its spring. When one had mustered courage enough and chanced to be alone in this place, the sudden and quite unexpected leaping to life of this bell would double the pulses. There was a distinct interval between the shock of its angry ring and the simple realization that this was only the postman—if indeed it was the postman! Out there unseen, by the front door, at a place where it was impossible to spy first, stood some stranger.

Here, startled by the loud sign he had given, was a child, gazing up to the dark ceiling and watching the vibrations and waggings of a bell on its spring. Maids were far off in the school kitchen, and it was not the custom for maids to answer our door. If somebody didn't soon come it would be my duty to turn the key and see who was there. The tingling of the bell grew kinder and quieter, it settled down to single rings, and even they lost at each shake the fury of their first sound. The bell on its spring soon grew tired. At last it was silent, though the shaking and leaping of the spring went on. Then, from the other end of the hall, came the click of the letter-box, and the fall of thirty letters in disorder on to the mat. So it *was* the postman, and I realized this with relief; for it could have been a tramp, a rough man asking for food, or a visitor to one of the boys, or a policeman—which once, to my horror, it had been. But as it was letters, there was nothing so very extraordinary about it. Letters came three times a day, and somebody was sure to come and fetch them soon.

What was I there for, then? Nothing needed me in the drawing-room; there was nobody in the little flagged hall, nobody on the stairs. I was there for the fascination of fear, as though I had dared my spirit to go on my legs to the front door and not be frightened. Or perhaps I did want something—a cardboard box or a piece of string—in that cupboard hiding behind me. Then I would take courage, with a delicious terror, and pull open the door of the cupboard under the stairs, where, in the dark, and among the dry smells of paper and packages, I would go down on my knees to search for the box or the cord I must have. And if I take a piece of cardboard to-day and break it and smell its dry scent, I am back in an instant on my knees among the surprising lumber of that cupboard, in haste for a nameless fear, searching for a box or a piece of string, alone; with the letters lying on the prickly mat at the hall door, and as yet nobody brave and grown up there to look them through.

I have found a box that will do.

Overhead, dulled by the ceiling, do you hear that slow rhythm of grind and squeak, grind and squeak, the grind shaking the house? It comes from the nursery, where Stella is riding the rocking-horse away. So I shut the door of the cupboard, and go down the one step and along the narrowest passage (I can easily touch both walls as I walk along) past the door on the left of the curtained and carpeted front dining-room, and up the steep backstairs with difficulty, to the door of the nursery at last.

I stop with my hand round the smallest door knob in the house, a children's size, the latch giving its characteristic rattle, a noise I should know in the dark. Stop then, before we enter. Now you can hear the hobby-horse plainly, the squeak of its hinges as the front legs dip, the clap of the yellow stand on the floor when its back legs rise; for Stella is riding him furiously now, to the time of the backwards and forwards rattle of the mysterious marble which someone once put in at the hole by the saddle. You have been in the room once before, you know. But then it was dark. The curtains were drawn round the door and round the window, and a lamp was burning on the wall above the fire. Then it was bathtime, and towels hung over the guard, ready for the next to come out of the water; and the hobby-horse stood in silence, munching the ghost of corn from an empty nosebag, stabled in the shadows, put by for the night.

6

The Day Nursery

FROM wainscot to ceiling the walls of our nursery were papered with pictures. Most of these were those large lithographs in many colours which used to be given away with *Pears' Annual*. They were stuck to the wall itself and varnished there, so that they were as much a part of the room as the walls and floor and window, and more permanent than the chairs and table, the toys and other movables. All of our pictures were peaceful and genial, domestic or quietly humorous scenes. If they did not tell a story to grown-ups we soon made them do so to us, for we took them into our lives with unquestioning frankness, accepting them as things not less permanent and objective than trees and roads and real people.

There was a complete absence of criticism, as I remember it, in our attitude to the established things of the world. We were thrown into a world which had all the appearance of permanence, and it did not occur to us to rearrange it. We drew a sharp line between pretence and reality; we would pretend about real things often enough, but we always held, at the same time, to the sane realities of things. The table with its table-cloth would serve for a lion's den—it was, indeed, a lion's den, and that without the slightest attempt at material disguises. Its darkness and its confined space (when you were underneath it) were all that we wanted, but for practical reasons its table-nature was not resented. The den and the table were two things, they existed together without jostling; a child might be painting with his box of paints, sitting at the table, and two children underneath might be Daniel and the Lions. Each party accepted the other party's interpretation of the table, as well as his own, without any difficulty.

We did not expect imagination to work through our senses, or by deception. Reason did not step in and say: This isn't a lion's den: this is a table. We knew it was a table to everyone; we were only just then employing these qualities which it shared with our conception of a lion's den, we were only pretending that it was a lion's den to us. But the game was in us, not in the table, and the most exact model of a rocky cave, though it would have delighted us, would not, I think, have satisfied us more, or made us feel more like Daniel and the Lions.

Pretending is a child's art alone, and grown-ups cannot practise it: they can only act. The pretender has no audience but himself: he is not trying to appear like the character he presents, he is that character and feels like it. If he has put a towel round the muzzle of the rocking-horse and is driving through rain and storm to catch a train, his feelings will be very nearly the real feelings which he would himself enjoy if the horse were a real horse, the towel a real bridle, the rain wet and the storm loud. But he will never be overcome by imagination; he will know, if you stop and ask him, that the bridle is a towel, the horse a wooden horse, and the rain nothing to you. Such pretence, which is with children an absorbing game, is with adults, except as something ludicrous, quite impossible. A child who is quite alone can sit on a chair and pretend, for a whole hour, to be the baker's man driving his cart. It is a glorious art, to which there are no limitations of subject at all. But a grown-up alone does not pretend at all without either deceiving himself (when he is insane) or shamefastly laughing. Only the child can see the two worlds side by side and seriously live at once by two standards, not complaining either that reality does not come up to imagination, or that imagination is false or foolish beside reality. When, for example, a child is drawing, drawing is a kind of pretence. You ask him what this square box is; he says it's a castle, and this conventional collection of lines is St George, and this the dragon he is killing. These quaint and intrinsically meaningless pencil lines are ridiculous and inadequate as representations of the things conceived, but the child is perfectly satisfied with them, because his imagination does not deal with sense impressions at all in detail. The extreme simplicity of the drawing may be related to the simplicity of the action in his mind, but these marks are only reminders. They don't bear, and the child never thought of making them bear, any nearer relation to the action. It is all so clear and rational: of course they are not *like* castles and knights, they are pencil and paper, pencil and paper all the time, proofs that the imagined action did have some real outcome—the movement of the pencil defining characteristic forms, the squareness of castles, the face and hands and legs of a knight, the spirit of that action expressed in the spirit of this entirely separate action, no more than the (outwardly imperfect) sympathy of hand and eye with the adventures of an extremely simple soul. If this be true, then the child is never an artist, because he makes no allowances for an audience or spectator. The simple drawing by one child makes no more appeal to another child than it does to the adult; and of course it makes less appeal than an elaborate representation by a grown-up artist. Childish pictures are rubbish to children. Only to himself, and only at the moment, is a child's own drawing adequate, because it is, like music to the composer, an active expression; but it is not a portrayal.

It is so easy to complicate simple matters. We all had our paint-boxes and our occasional furies for drawing, on wet days, but we never dreamed of any connection between our hieroglyphs and the pictures on the nursery wall. To all the long processes of which those pictures were the result we were, naturally, indifferent. To us they were not drawn, but printed. Whatever that might mean to one who knew, it simply meant to us that they existed in their own right, independent of any human originator, printed pictures were pictures as roads were roads— they were not windows but objects; at least, that is how I now remember their effect upon us. There was, for example, a picture of a butcher's boy, a Victorian ragamuffin of a boy, who had sat himself down on the stone steps of a great house to read a paper called *Tit Bits*. He had left his basket of chops and steaks meanwhile on the bottom step, and here a dog was stealing them while he read. We saw the fun of this, though I must confess that, till this moment, I never saw the significance of the name of the paper; but we did not see the boy as a boy, nor follow out the consequences of his neglect.

There was another picture, one, I believe, of a

series called the Five Senses. This, which we had, was Tasting, and showed what I now think must have been two fat monks, one tasting from a dish of macaroni. We held that it was a man eating pickled cabbage. Macaroni never came our way, but red cabbage did—and in such quantities as the piled dish of the monk held. For Catherine, in the long dark school kitchen, would spend whole afternoons, in season, in cutting crisply through the hard red hearts of cabbage from the garden, slicing them into long purple strips which turned blue later on in the salt with which they were sprinkled. There we had seen such piles as this; had smelt the smell of boiling vinegar with ginger in it, and very well knew the reason for the smile on the fat round face of the monk in our picture. He tasted with a spoon in his hand, from which the strings of food hung down; his other hand lay satisfactorily spread upon his lower chest. His picture was pasted high up at the north end of the west wall.

Of the thirty pictures which must have adorned our nursery, only a few now remain clear in memory: two in particular (besides those I have just mentioned) remained my favourites and, so far as I have gathered, the favourites of all of us. On the chimney-piece was a gay and lively winter scene with skaters. It seems to me that there were a good many figures in those flying, leaning postures which, though still, impress a feeling of graceful gliding motion on the mind; but of all this crowd only one person now presents herself clearly to memory. This is the figure of a girl in a red dress trimmed with white fur; her hands are hidden in a tiny round muff, and she is also wearing a white fur cap, and I know I remember this girl with easy delight because one of my cousins was the proud possessor of a muff of white fur. We argued among ourselves, too, about the identity of the other people in the picture, and really entered into the winter sport with enthusiasm. Our greatest delight, however, was always to find names for the figures—not names alone either, but definite personalities. We had a large number of aunts and uncles and schoolmasters and cousins in our lists, and we drew upon these freely. One point of resemblance, one detail of costume, was enough to give them a name that we all knew.

As for this snow picture, I think I can find two reasons for its popularity, in addition to the wonderful discovery of the muff. One is mine in particular: simply that it reminded me of the days when I lived at Hor-Den, when I fell asleep dreaming of such scenes. One is general: it is that snow in the country has a special and highly romantic appeal of its own. Healthy children, such as we were, come to no harm in it; and we loved to be allowed to exercise the courage that was in us, for a certain amount of bodily courage was needed to face the cold at first. But snow's appeal was really almost the appeal of magic. If you could go to sleep on a winter's night and wake up to a May morning, the sudden transformation would not be more astonishing, nor more delightful, than the transformation of a fall of snow. In a night, in a couple of hours, the whole character of the world, without labour or noise or revolution, is completely changed. There is a Lewis Carroll rhyme in *Sylvie and Bruno* which says:

> He thought he saw a rattlesnake
> Which spoke to him in Greek;
> He looked again and found it was
> The middle of next week....

Upon the routine of ordinary day-of-the-week life, snow silently descends to change it. The change that it works comes quicker than the rhythm of normal change. You can watch your usual Thursday occupations gradually buried by a fall of snow, and I can well recall the intense and growing excitement of us children as we watched the swirl of flakes (which we always called the feathers of the geese which Mother Goose was plucking) and eagerly prophesied to one another how soon it would settle thickly. In a good fall, the first great change is quick.

You leave the window and run to the fire, then you look again and find, to your surprise, that it is the middle of next week. The lagging Spirit of Time is beaten, the world is given over to supernatural change. With snow about you cannot do ordinary things: to-day is not to-day.

If the snow were wet, or still falling, so that we knew we could not go out, we would lean all together on the low nursery window-sill, staring out across the road to the orchard, our eyes made dizzy by the constant slow flakes as they floated down and by to settle. Four pairs of eyes were not enough to notice all, nor four excited voices enough to announce all the novelties, the birds that flew down, the solitary waggon that drew by, the depth of the snow in the wheel-tracks, or in the scoop-shaped laurel leaves immediately underneath us, or how it piled up against the window-glass, or how the millions of grey specks fought one another in the sky above the elm tops. We lived then, except for our mere bodies, in the world outside; games and books and fire were all forgotten while we gave our souls over to the snow. But by and by the flakes would stop falling, the cold would harden, the creation of the new world with its new planes and levels would be completed, and then we would dance round our mother with our "Can-we-go-out-

and-play-in-the-snow" tune, a specially persuasive wheedling question. So she would wisely consult with our father, whose decision in these matters was always founded on profound knowledge of the qualities of weather and snow, and then we would oil our boots with melted dripping, put on scrubby woollens, and open the door.

There at the very door was the snow, with marks of the feet of privileged grown-ups leading to us and away from us, where the black ground showed through in a variety of shoe shapes. The wonder of it, the nearness now, the whiteness, the brightness, the way you screwed your eyes up, the tidyness of the world! At first it was pleasure enough just to walk on it, feeling your feet sink in, and the squeak and crunch of your steps; then to run, careless whether you were on path or grass, the great delight being to make your tracks in snow that had not been imprinted before, to run scattering and then to stop and look back at the way you had written in the snow. Once, I remember, we looked over a gate with a great sloping field as white as a giant's sheet of notepaper, and we climbed into this field and ran wildly, writing our names with our feet in giant letters for the sky to read; then, starting with a small ball of snow at the top of the slope, we rolled it over and over, the snowball growing so fast as we rolled it that it soon needed more help than one could give, and at the last steep slope a sphere of snow half as high as our heads took to its own motion and lurched forward heavily, and lodged, a giant, in the ditch where we were forced to let it lie.

The sky was darker than the land; indoors through windows the light struck upwards to the ceiling instead of downwards to the floor; out of doors our hands and faces looked brown and rosy in contrast with the whiteness of the snow; our voices had no echoes, our games, our world, our characters were all necessarily different from those of the ordinary week-day world. There was nothing that the miracle did not change, and nothing, however trivial, which was not impressed with twice its normal significance upon minds intoxicated with the white excitement. So it was then, and so it is to-day; for if the truth be told there is a child in every one when snow is about, and the word *snow* is richer in youthful associations than almost any other English word. We children had good reason to like to turn again and again to that winter scene pasted above our nursery fireplace; it was a picture of one of the intensest joys of our exciting lives.

The other well-remembered picture was in a summer season. It was of two girls ("ladies" we called them) climbing up a ladder, one behind the other, to look over a wall. I don't know what particular reason, according to the painter or the title, was supposed to bid them there; but it was a natural thing to do. If people will put up walls, curiosity will look over them. At a place not far from us there was a large country estate completely shut in by a twelve-foot wall. Behind this wall a madman lived, as, thanks to good nursemaids, we very well knew, and indeed the wall made it easy to believe. We never saw the other side of that wall; a complete piece of reality was thus shut off from our senses, but our curiosity was only doubled by the wall's opposition, and over those unrealized acres (with the mad rich man thrown in) our imaginations held large and reckless sway. The mad unseen was, indeed, a terror; and I doubt if I should have had the courage to walk the long road past this wall alone; but terror, safe from actual danger, I ever found a goad to the imagination.

These two ladies, then, were looking over their wall. All that they could see was hidden from us by tree-tops, but there was a tip-toe eagerness about them, which suggested that what they were hoping to see was not yet in sight. We used to tell each other that they were up early, and the reason shows a curious piece of childish logic. These girls were dressed in fashions that we could not recognize. Their hair was in loose piles about and above their heads, and they wore what looked to us like Miss Richardson's corsets outside their dresses. As the only time when these garments were ever seen by us was well before breakfast, we concluded that these girls had not finished dressing or doing their hair. They must have been in a hurry we thought. They were up to mischief, that was certain, and what time was freer for mischief than the early morning? The profile of one, and the fair fuzzy hair done up loosely, somehow reminded us of one of our aunts, and this lady, like the lady who tickled the kittens in a picture at grandfather's Farm, was known and treated as Aunt Lydia.

Most vivid of all pictures, however, was a mere portrait, not in our nursery at all, but hanging downstairs in the breakfast-room, next to a watercolour of peaches. It was a portrait of a lady again, notable for three reasons; for her strange coiffure (the Regency style, I believe), for her supposed likeness to a fair girl whom we saw every Sunday at Chapel, and for a pictorial effect so startling to us that it seemed to be the work of magic: for wherever you stood, her eyes were upon you, watching; worse than this, if you kept looking at the picture as you walked across the room, her eyes followed you, and although the expression on her face remained un-altered you felt that you were in the room, not with a picture, but with a person; that behind those following eyes was an intent and critical mind. We called this portrait Miss Meadows, after the lady of the Chapel.

Those other pictures in the nursery did not much disturb us, they never excited our imaginations so that we could forget that they were pictures; but in the more grown-up and restricted air of the breakfast-room, pictures were less familiar friends, and perhaps that is why we treated Miss Meadows as a person. She was a power, and the measure of her power is that we all remember her so well; for her portrait, like all the rest of the pictures of those days, has long ago disappeared.

They were poor art, but we cared little for that. When we first knew them, because we had come to them and found them there already, we treated them as things established, beyond criticism, needing no justification, and likely to be there for ever. When the old nursery was abandoned and made into a bedroom, we tried with water and a knife to remove the pictures from the walls to save them, but the paste and varnish were too strong for us. At length they were covered over by wall-paper, and yet, among the stirring excitements of such changes, it was impossible not to feel regret: and not by any means out of a sentimental regard for our old pictures, but because this change, like the cutting down of the wood, struck hard at our natural belief in the permanence of the world. The tremor struck deep which began in such an insignificant way; the walls of our nursery were going now, and we felt, though still dimly, the shadow of the gnomon, our whispered mortality. There was something to resent and to fear when time, touching simple things, touched the solid world about us, and faith had to be begun again.

7

Grandfather's Early Days

HE was seventy-three when he died, and I was only ten: ten knows little of seventy-three. They put a memorial tablet on the wall of the Chapel that he had built, and hung a large picture of him in the vestry there; a fund of money was raised by his old pupils to perpetuate his name, the interest it bore to be devoted, not unsuitably, to yearly prizes for Common Sense, of which, I should think, he had his share.

His mind was made up; that, I feel, looking at his portrait, is the first thing to say of him. It is remarkable how little he alters with time in all the photographs we have. The earliest was taken in 1869; its "properties"—its tumbled curtain falling into one corner over a carved table-edge on which documents are lying—show that even then, and even in photography, the tradition of Sir Joshua Reynolds was not quite dead. But the documents, like the table and the curtain, belonged to the photographer. Grandfather was not the man to leave important papers lying about on tables. He looks out at me exactly as he looked out at the photographer, who, in spite of all merely professional polish, had an immortal soul. My grandfather therefore looked at the photographer, and not, as instructed, at the cold unspiritual eye of the camera. He was not the man to be frightened into a strange mood, or cowed by science. On the other hand, the photographer, even in his own studio, must have felt a little disturbed and uneasy because his usually successful professional ways could not tackle this gentleman from the country.

"I am not a subject, and you are not a photographer," say my grandfather's eyes, looking out of the year 1869. "I am a man and you are a man: here we two are in this room together, and I wonder what you are doing with your life. Are you, like so many, careless of the treasure entrusted to you? Do you think of yourself as nothing but a photographer, a man in a hard world, or as an immortal soul? Ah, that's the question, that's it, that's it. Don't let my look confuse you," he says, "you must—men must—do the job in hand. Do it well, and I will pay you for it. But life is a battle, it is so much more than the taking of photographs. Seventy years of it, seventy years, and it doesn't end then with death! And there lies your problem, and every man's. Once," says my grandfather's thought, "once it was my problem too. I was young then; but I praise heaven

72

—(he holds a book firmly on his crossed knees, with both hands gripping it, and I can almost fancy that I see him tap it on his knee)—I say I praise heaven for this blessed book, where all men's problems are made clear. Do you know this book? For twenty years (he was 38) I have studied in it warnings, promises, adjurations, homilies; with devotion, with prayer, with fear, with joy deeper than I can express. It has never failed me in my needs; it never will fail me. It would not fail you. Oh make it the foundation on which you will build your life!"

I hope it will not be thought an exaggeration for me to deduce as much as this from an old and fading photograph. In every hour of his intercourse with people such thoughts and anxieties and assurances as these were in his mind. As he was a man, he must have had his doubts and moral failures; but from the time when, as a young weaver in London, he considered of it and accepted the authority of the Bible, to the very moment of his death, he never changed his mind. For every judgment he had this one reliable assay, which nothing could refute. Oil and water were more easily mixed than right and wrong in his mind. Gain, expediency, politeness, carelessness, or comfort, could not move him from his purpose an inch; for why, the purpose was not his, but God's, and you cannot compromise with God.

73

If I am right in thus interpreting his bearing to the world, it is no great wonder that so little of his human character has been told to me. He was an institution and had become a tradition, long before he died; not only to us children, which would not have been remarkable in any man of his comparatively great age, but to his grown-up sons and daughters, our parents, aunts and uncles; so that in all the talk that ever reached our ears we did not hear one word of criticism.

He would come and pay his morning call, on his rounds of inspection, and we would see him sometimes. I speak with reverence, for he did us grave honour—to us it was rather like receiving a friendly visitor from Olympus. He was kind, and remotely playful; he would stoop to smile in at us, and draw a peppermint circle from his black waistcoat pocket, snap it in half across the line of letters that said EXTRA STRONG, and give each child a piece. He spoke very slowly, and you felt that he comprehended and classified you. "Now, I won-der," he would say, "I won-der if we could find anything in this pocket for Frank." But it was only the rhetoric of omniscience. He did not speak *to* you, but spoke about you in your hearing. If it was a rainy day, he would playfully complain that the rain was spoiling all his little potatoes. It was so unlike him to complain, that here you ought to show surprise, whereupon he would gently add that "it was turning them all into big ones." Or if it was a bright day, he would begin with a pet name for this child and a pet saying for that. To me he would repeatedly recite the nursery rhyme that begins:

> Frank, Frank,
> The butter's rank,
> The cheese has all gone mouldy.

I find I have little recollection of him as a person; there was no flash between us; the fun was all on his side really, and, although we appreciated his gracious ways to us, we did not joke with him. To play tricks with him would have been unthinkable: you cannot think of snowballing a phenomenon, and he was a phenomenon in our world, as certain as the morning, as constant and as calculable, and because he had always been an established office in the world to which we were born, we accepted him, as we accepted the nursery pictures, without thought or question.

I remember the kind of coat that he wore—a smooth black alpaca—and in the photograph of 1869, taken long before any of us were born or thought of (as my mother would say), I am not surprised to find that he was even then wearing the same kind of coat. In that portrait, too, he holds a book on his knees; so he does, and crosses his legs too, in a portrait taken thirty years later. In both the mouth is the same, long and generous, but narrow and very firm, though not hard. The early portrait shows a sympathetic and slightly humorous pair of eyes, in it he wears the look of a man whose faith is a vigorous optimism; in the later portraits there is a graver look, and the eyes would be sad or disappointed, if to be sad or disappointed were not to cast a slight upon the faith he still held. The early look of confidence has changed a little, and I think I can detect the influence on character which undisputed power seems to produce on even the kindliest of men: a hardening of good nature, when men begin to take refuge in the abstract and iron idea of justice, lest their kindness should lead them to relax, and the principles to which they are loyal should suffer in consequence. For obstinacy is a family characteristic of ours, and it looks as if grandfather had it in his composition.

Perhaps he made up his mind a little too early and a little too definitely, and had to be obstinate in maintaining that position in the face of experience. Perhaps he was too proud to admit disillusion: his older face sometimes looks sad and stern. Yet we children did not think him so, and we were never afraid of him, because, as I have said, he was so certain, so consistent, in his clothes, his morning visits, his benevolence, his third person manner of addressing you, his rhymes and his peppermints. One day, however, he was different.

It was in the summer holidays. Some building alterations were going on at the school, and among the builder's materials was a large heap of beautiful brown rounded pebbles, brought straight from the seashore. John and Stella and I had found this heap, and we were enjoying ourselves, using pebbles as David did when he went out against Goliath, only our goliaths were invented: empty tins sometimes, or sparrows. We were so small that our throwing could do no harm—we certainly thought of none—when along came grandfather on his morning visit, inspecting the alterations and the gardens. We did not stop or suffer any guilty fear at all. I think we quite expected to hear him murmur to the oak-tree near by: "And what, I won-der, shall we find in our pocket for John and Stella and Frank?" Instead, he sharply ordered us to stop, in a firm commanding voice which did not seem to belong to him at all, and thus completely overthrew our sanguine preparations for soft words of play and possible peppermints.

It was not a very stern rebuke, and certainly it was necessary. We stopped at once, not in fear or guilt (for I remember the effect very plainly), but in astonishment. It hurt us to feel that grandfather had acted out of character. Even if we had been feeling at all guilty we should hardly have expected or understood displeasure from him; but we had played in innocence, and we were doubly perplexed. What annoyed him was the waste of good pebbles; but we had just been to the seaside, and did not know that pebbles were of any value.

"Now, now, you mustn't do that!" he said, "you mustn't do that. Your father would be very angry. You must go at once and pick up all the stones that you have thrown away, and put them all back on the heap."

We had thrown hundreds, and we knew that he was asking something absurd; but we obeyed in silence, shocked by disillusion. But this shock was only of short effect. The cutting down of the wood had compelled us to retreat from an old position and reshape our opinions about woods. This we had done reluctantly, it is true, but there for a continual reminder was the palpable evidence, the denuded wood, day in and day out for more than a year. But this lapse into peccant humanity on grandfather's part was only for a moment. The next day when he met us, all was as if it had never happened, rhymes and peppermints were just as usual, and we eagerly took back to our hearts the image of him that had been there so long. I never saw him displeased again.

For a portrait of him as he seemed to me while he moved about this little country kingdom of his during the six or seven years when his figure was familiar to me, you must see a neat old gentleman with a snow-white beard and smiling eyes, a solidly built and rather heavy figure, with blunt and very shiny boots, long unrumpled and intensely black trousers, black waistcoat with watch-guard of silk or horsehair, light black and half glossy alpaca coat, and a low-crowned big brimmed black hat.

Into the gait of this rather sombre figure now coming down the path from the Farm it is easy to read seriousness of purpose (without solemnity), a strong will in the tread, in the lack of swing a strict guard; but above all a quiet happiness and confidence (such as the music of Bach expresses) which, finding no other bodily outlet, gives itself away by a peculiar springing step, where each heel raises itself eagerly before the dignified leg moves on in measured pace. Grandfather, if I hazard a guess, was sometimes in the habit of singing to himself when he walked alone.

I cannot remember a word of his sermons, nor even what kind of sermon he preached, though

I must have listened to a hundred or so. I can remember his figure there on the platform. I sat near to the platform (which was fenced round like a little balcony) so that my eyes were on a level with the toes of grandfather's shiny boots. Up above these boots rose the reading desk, which it was his habit to hold firmly with both hands, bending his elbows outwards. I don't think he used his hands at all in preaching. Anyhow, his voice went out into the air well above me; and it seems to me that I followed his sermons by watching his boots. They fascinated me; his feet were planted close together, pointing at me; and as he preached, and specially as he offered up his prayers, I could see that he swung and heaved his body by his hands—it was a firm and solid reading desk of pitch pine that he grasped—and, as the fervour of his exhortation rose and fell, he went up on tip-toe or sunk to heels again.

The body feels and would express what the heart is feeling; a quick impulsive nature will use quick impulsive gestures; humour, action, narrative will be in the body as well as in the words. A reasoning man, or one who loves intellectual analysis, will shape and tear and mould and unfold and smooth down his invisible subject with his fingers; but grandfather clung with all his quiet strength to the solidity of the desk before him, subdued his bodily sympathies until the currents of feeling that flowed in him were all but invisible to his congregation. He tip-toed in intensity of purpose, and slightly swayed his body, and that was all.

When he prayed, he threw back his head, and spoke, I thought, as though Someone were listening at the fretwork ventilator in the roof of the Chapel. His eyes were shut, but one day, when I ventured to watch him at prayer, I found to my astonishment that the lids were not closed, and I could see the white part of his eyes. It had a strange and ghastly effect; we tried, among ourselves, to imitate it in the nursery, but it was very difficult.

His prayers were conversations, without any sort of pulpit manner, except that his phrases, from long practice, must have fallen easily into the most familiar shapes. His intensity was never merely intensity of voice, accent, gesture, manner—it was unmistakable indubitable faith, faith so strongly held and so constantly that it had acquired all the assurance of knowledge. He was a quiet man, but then his strength was in quietness.

I have raised his spirit with difficulty, but at last he almost stands behind me—a grave and noble ancestor, just, stern but gentle-hearted. White-headed and white-bearded, with something of a patriarchal dignity—in face, but not in figure;

an oracle respected by his relatives; one not easily understood by children, but a calm and secure comforter to sad people, and himself a radiant and happy man. He lived for 73 years, guided, he would say, by God; and who shall dispute it, or wrangle now with new definitions of God?

When he began, he began in the wildest improvidence of faith. At seventeen he was converted. I can only wish that we had some authentic story of his struggling, one would like to know more of his battles than the victories. He was a silk-weaver (and the son of a silk-weaver), living in Bethnal Green; and as he belonged to the poorer people he had little education, and very soon a great deal of work to do. But he attended evening classes, and when he had learned he began to teach.

By twenty-three he had married, and was giving up one working day a week to visiting and preaching. "I had," he said, "a great yearning desire to bring souls to Christ." So great a desire it was, and so constant, that, after eight years of waiting and learning, he suddenly threw up his livelihood, and without any guarantee (as the business man would say) started a day school, a Sunday school, and a church, in Globe Street, Mile End. After three years of this he reports himself: "I am not tired of serving God, nor tired of the work he sets me; no, nor tired of the way in which he provides for me."

When he had a son and daughter, and while they were both infants, his wife died. This was in 1859. She had been a wife to him in his work as well as in his family, but he struggled on alone for more than a year. In 1861 he broke down in health and was ordered three months' rest in the country. How casually the doctor may have spoken of it: just three months' rest, and in the country, he said, with no notion that he was the mouthpiece of destiny. But grandfather could not afford to be idle for three months. He obtained a letter of introduction to the "Country Towns Missions." When he called on the secretary he found him reading a letter, just arrived, from a place called "Finchcocks" at Gowdhurst, asking for a man to be sent to the place for three months, to hold meetings during harvest and hop-picking.

"Gowdhurst," says my grandfather (though only in my imagination), trying over on his tongue a strange name of no associations whatever. "And where is Gowdhurst?"

He accepted the job, and went alone. He was to be back in three months, when the job (and the pay) would finish; but he never went back.

Somewhere between the ages of seventeen and thirty he had made one profoundly important step in the dark. This was the willing submission to Biblical authority. The Bible henceforward was to be his one fixed authority; not in any magical sense, but as a store of inspired wisdom where the wise interpreter might find clear guidance for every decision he would have to make, and a way to order his life in the uncertain darkness of the world. Such a step of faith taken, as I say, wilfully, and by a man whose pride was his firmness of purpose, now for ever fixed his attitude to the adventures of life. At the age of thirty therefore he calmly decided to throw himself and his family upon the mercies of God; not to work for a livelihood, but to work and expect his living. Providence was not a mere euphemism for God; authority said simply, among other things: "The Lord will provide."

"Very well," said my grandfather, "I'll trust in Providence," and exchanged the visible for an invisible means of support, found that there was work enough for a lifetime in Gowdhurst, sent for his two children, and settled down to do it.

He proceeded by study (which was not very congenial to him, I imagine) to justify his acceptance; and though he must have had his moments of perplexity, his days and weeks of it, perhaps, he found at last that no experience succeeded in shaking his first faith. He believed in the inspiration of the Bible, literally and simply (and disbelieved in the Pope), more than anyone does to-day.

8

Grandfather at Gowdhurst

So grandfather arrived at Gowdhurst. In spite of his spirit, the work in London had made him tired. Because of his passion for the saving of souls, numbers overwhelmed him. He saw millions of struggling human creatures without leisure for any hope except the hope of living on. What mark could his greatest effort make in such a turmoil? How, among all its despairs, could he do his best? Except in strongest natures, love of mankind may become, in such a crowd, a useless hunger, self-despised and in danger of impotence. He worked there for six years; but even in saying "I am not tired," it seems as if he is covering up some weariness. His wife died and left him without a comrade. He looked that loneliness in the eyes for two more years, till his body failed under the burden which his spirit bent it to bear. Then being sent to the country, he found that the energy which only seemed to waste itself in London was sufficient to make some impression upon the country people. He could see what he did in the country, he could remember, he could learn, he could perceive by its effects that his faith was justified, and that his love was a power. The quietness gave him time to think; the number of souls was within count; he could make his passion felt here.

He was a born Londoner, and I do not know that the different beauty of the country touched him deeply or constantly, but he must have been glad of the countenance of quietness, and particularly so, because out of that comfort he found strength renewed for his work. Of his vocation, once heard, he never seems to have entertained a doubt; nor did he change his purpose by coming into the country. He did not retire to think about God, or to commune with the soul of Nature, as philosophers have done; he was not running away from humanity when he left the city, but began at once to make new friends and new communities of friends, to hold meetings and a school, laying out this garden for a life's labour.

He brought his children to the country too, and in a year or two he married again, taking the sister of his first wife. He held meetings anywhere, in cottages and in barns and in the meadows, and by the end of the year he had organized no less than five small communities, which it now became his duty to serve. He walked from place to place, doing this self-appointed work, giving the country people his own thoughts about God just as he dug them for himself from the mines of scripture, and always relating his own experiences with the austere authority of simple truth.

By borrowing a barn he began a school; twopence a week for every child taught was the fee he asked, and there are still men and women, old and breaking now, who first learnt their letters here at his charge. My grandfather, I have heard it said, was no born teacher. He lived without theories, certainly without any theories of education; but a man who can read is better than a man who can't, and in teaching a child to spell and to count, as my grandfather very well knew, chances arise to teach as well whatever may seem to the teacher's mind to be of more vital importance. You may teach him to pray, to be kind, to be clean and neat, to be methodical and careful and serious; for twopence a week you may teach him to read, and without extra charge you may teach him to grow up. This, I feel sure, was my grandfather's way. Much of the modern wild experimental education, with its careful avoidance of discipline, and its attempts to avert growing up, he would have condemned as mischievous nonsense— as sentimental, if the word had been possible to him.

While he hammered away at making ends meet, he belittled this life and the world in which it must be lived, by the magnificent vision of a life to come in a world to come. Magnificent is the word, for the glories of heaven, in the words of those who would have us desire it, sound either incredibly different from the warm and mortal pleasures (and these glories are the visions of gold and light and music), or safely and impalpably abstract, glorious and ineffable, a blaze of bliss of which we only know that it is unlike the fragile loves and joys of this despised world. Mystics are few; grandfather was not a mystic; yet somehow or other the heaven that he felt like a promise to himself, what he thought to be the spring of his motives, was, as he would have put it, "to be with Jesus." The phrase has been shouted at us and sung at us and spoilt for us in a thousand ways by vague people sick of their own emotions. A simple heart will not shudder. If I am myself shut out from the ecstasy, yet I know two things well: that my grandfather was virile, hale and sincere in his manhood, a practical and likeable fellow; and that he wore his religion naturally and easily, without any loss of his vigour or perversion of his pride or bright human affection. These mountains that I see, his faith easily removed. He made himself, by hope of heaven, independent of earthly happiness, and was earthly happy in his independence.

The twopenny school and the preaching became important at that outer part of Gowdhurst which I have described as our hill of sand. There was on this hill a well-to-do squire farmer, a gruff old fellow of the old school, who took it into his head to help my grandfather, when the barn which had been both school and church was destroyed. He helped to provide a building which might be used without interruption, and in 1866 my grandfather began to consider himself by profession a schoolmaster, though by calling still a preacher. The rest of the story is only of the growth of his school and his church on this hill. For he prospered, as sober solid English nonconformists will; the building of a national school near by relieved him of his twopenny scholars, and boarding pupils began to arrive.

It would be foolish to pretend that this nucleus of a school was admirable or perfect. My grandfather was no scholar, to begin with, and no child psychologist. His discipline was summary, not persuasive. He was teacher, guardian, preceptor and doctor to the boys who were sent to him. No doubt he knew the proverb which says that boys will be boys, but I think he rather disliked this natural habit of theirs. Boys will be men, was more in his prophecy.

There is a story of a boy who was sick, for whom grandfather prepared the usual stiff dose of physic.

But by some misfortune he remembered the wrong name and called up a boy who was in perfect health. It speaks plainly of grandfather's way, that the medicine was taken, though by the wrong boy. The life was Spartan, and murmurs were silenced with firmness. A pump to wash at, a bed to sleep on, a room to work in, a wood to play in, the plainest of food, no sort of organized games, no touch of art anywhere, few books but Bibles, no music but hymns, no culture but religion, for reason rules, for holidays long walks—these were the characteristics, and in the hands of a rogue the school might have been a scandal.

In a dormitory one moonlight night, late enough to seem perfectly safe, a youth with a turn for satire was giving an undisciplined imitation of my grandfather. "This is old Kayzey," he said; and touched on all the points of manner and character with relish and with that crude bitterness of which some boys are capable. When he had finished, earlier than he need have done because of an uncanny reserve in the boys who watched him, he turned to find my grandfather close beside him. No word passed then or afterwards. This was about the time of that earliest portrait, and my grandfather has humorous eyes.

On Saturdays pocket money was given out to the

scholars. Then my grandfather would do on a black holland apron, with the coppers in a pocket in front, and the boys lined up on the grass to receive their pence. One ingenious fellow, having taken his money at the head of the line, slipped out behind and stood in the line again lower down. He thought the old gentleman would never notice. It was poor character reading, for grandfather was a careful man; when he came opposite to the scamp, and while his hand was even going to the apron pocket for the coins, grandfather looked and remembered. He said nothing; but the boy (so Barratt says) went down like a log. I daresay he didn't, for grandfather was not a brute; but legend or not, the story shows the man truly. He could hate cunning or dishonesty, as though it was a personal enemy. His anger was sudden; but his habit of mind was just.

It will be gathered from this that he was a stern parent. I cannot, for obvious reasons, tell much of his family life. Very early in their lives the two children of his first wife were put to work to help with the teaching in the twopenny school. My father was the eldest son of the second family, and he began to teach at the age of fourteen or fifteen. They kept a maid or two at school to do some of the work, but no servant of the family; housework, cooking, cleaning, churning were all done by my grandmother (who managed the domestic affairs of the school, too, at this time) with the help of her children. They were a large family and there was no time for idleness, and above all no habit of luxury, or money to spare and spend on comforts. In gardening, building, carpentry, paperhanging and decorating my father was soon an expert. It fell to his lot to make the very desks and forms at which his pupils sat. He taught them, and he made their furniture, and organized the newly permitted football and cricket, so that by eighteen or so he was quite grown up. His boyhood was short, his responsibility began very early, and by twenty-three he, too, was married and ready to manage the school. So grandfather bought the Farm, and went to live there, and my mother (who is still a girl) came back from her honeymoon holiday to find herself housekeeper for fifty or sixty.

My tireless grandfather had not only built a chapel in order to set free the old building for school alone, but had also opened a girls' school for the better employment of his elder daughters, and, as this prospered like the other, in a few years he purchased land two miles away in Gowdhurst village proper, and there put up a larger and better building. He bought a farm too, a hundred acres of hops and fruit, pasture and woodland; and finding, I suppose, that his children took work off his hands, at the age of sixty or so he turned farmer. London, by this time, was quite shaken off, except that grandfather never followed the custom of country squires to ride to their work. He kept a horse, but not to ride. From one school to another, and from either to the farm that he had bought (called Hor-Den), he trotted about along the country lanes in a four-wheeled, low-hung and thoroughly Victorian chaise. His short square figure flourishing the whip was a familiar sight in all these lanes thirty years ago, before anything more dangerous than a steam traction-engine had ever been seen on them. In those days even the steam traction-engine was preceded by a man carrying a red flag, as I have seen.

So grandfather trotted about, and the first pony of his that I remember was Charlie, a chestnut with fair mane and tail. By the time that I had begun to notice this horse, the best of his work was done, and soon he was relieved from work altogether and left to idle and grow fat in the fields, where he passed his time happily browsing over the hazel hedges of the cricket meadow, or chasing and cornering the sheep. Then Jack was bought. He was a comical piebald pony of astonishing roundness, and a horse with more intelligence than was always convenient; for corn in a hat would not avail to catch him in the paddock, and he learned all about the degrees of good

93

nature in his drivers specially to take advantage of
them, to crawl along or stand still on hills just as
long as saved him from a beating. He was strong,
and trotted well enough with a determined driver
behind him. Grandfather's custom was to get out
and walk beside the trap—we called it the trap—up
all the hills, and we would often meet him at Worms
Hill or Summer Hill or coming up past the sand-pits
from Hor-Den. We children would be out with our
nursemaid, and grandfather would stop the pony,
put on the brake, and give us each half a peppermint
from his pocket. Sometimes we might even ride
home with him, sitting on the buttoned cushions
beside him and swinging our short legs into the well
of the trap. But this was long before the days of
rubber tyres and tarred roads, and the wheels
scrunched over the gritty road, the trap swayed and
sank when grandfather stood up to flick the whip,
the shafts and fore-carriage squeaked at the turning
of corners, the harness creaked and clinked, the
shoes of Jack rang sharp on the metalled road, the
brisk air drove by our faces, carrying the smells
of horse, leather and dust; and now and then, on
birthdays, or if you were the only child in the trap,
grandfather would give you the ribbons to hold
while he got out and walked by Jack's side up the
long last hill.

For the railway station, for visits, for sermons abroad and for birthday picnics, Jack and the four-wheeler were always needed; and once, I remember, with Bess and a dog-cart in addition, all that there was of the family as yet went out in a body for a long drive through park gates and unfamiliar pastures, with food in parcels hidden away to have when the time came, and all in celebration of my mother's birthday.

9

Tea at the Farm

MUCH of this account has necessarily been made by knowledge and not by memory; all my grandfather's early history was unknown to us until his death; but although it was not at first intended to give more than a light and childish sketch of him as he touched us in those early days, he would not be kept out. He was essential to the world which I am recalling. More than half of the world into which we were born was of his making: the geography of it indeed was the other God's doing, and had a deeper and older history, the hills and streams (of which we somehow felt he was a contemporary) were hereabout when grandfather first came to Gowdhurst, a Londoner. We had that advantage over him: he saw them first when he was thirty years old, but our eyes opened on them. I know he did not change the country, and I cannot suppose that he made much real alteration in the countrymen and their women. The new things, the reading and the praying, which he came to impart, were hardly more than a slight polish upon a learning to which they were born and bred.

A woodman, making a copse fence, cuts a few stakes and drives them into the bank; then he weakens any near-by sapling with a blow from his bill, and bends the young living tree down, to weave it in and out among the stakes. So he goes on, down the whole length of the hedge, till he has woven a strong and continuous wattle the full length of the copse, and the weft of his wattle is living wood still growing rooted in the ground. City artisans may laugh, and say there is no skill in country labour, but they cannot tell how to make a fence that grows stronger as it grows older. Our country boys know a hundred matters of this kind before they have left school at fourteen. They will stare if you ask them where they learned such things, because they cannot remember learning. The thousand details of subtle technical knowledge, and the thousand skills in the use of such tools as axe, and scythe and bagging hook, would fill volumes for townsmen to read; but they are never written down. Woodcraft, hay-making, harvesting, gardening, thatching, stock-breeding, shepherding, poaching, will each afford many other examples. All civilization is hung on the back of such husbandry; it began when men gave up hunting and took to growing and rearing their food. Cain and Abel were the founders of modern society; nor have chemistry nor biology, nor all the engines of the ingenious been able to cut off the race of men from their dependence upon earth and these simpletons that know how to cultivate her. These skills are as much inherited as learned, and they go back deeper than history.

The countrymen's sins were as old as their virtues. I think that my grandfather was sorry for their ignorance, and angry perhaps at the light way the young ones held their consciences; but he knew that their sins were small beside their virtues; he soon found out that their ignorance was slight, too, against the vast body of their native knowledge; and did he not depend and live for a time upon their kindness? They hate a lie; they are entirely honest, except in the purely artificial matter of poaching; they may not be plain livers and high thinkers, but they are industrious, manly and simple. And though the standards of their youth may sometimes be crude, they are, almost without exception, faithful spouses and good and wise parents. The women work as hard as the men, too, on the farm in haymaking and hop-picking seasons, and in their homes in all seasons. Their homes are clean as honour, by tradition, and in spite of rather primitive conditions. They are a race of folk that Morris would have used to people his Utopia, for they love work, and die when they can work no longer.

No, grandfather did not come to teach them new virtues, though he helped them, perhaps, to foster those they had, and gave them, however narrowly, a glimpse of worlds of which they had too little hint before his time. But as they were human he loved these people, and in their slow and faithful way they answered him. When their kin died in the course of nature, he helped them to bear with nature. He married them, blessed them, and now and then buried them; but above all, his presence was a cheerful reminder of the goodness of life, a kind of comfort very welcome to those whose days grew dull sometimes with the heaviness of hard labour.

He did not alter the woods and fields, nor these, their old and rooted inheritors; but he made a great difference, for he brought down upon this remote hill a colony of strangers, a stream of boys from other parts, mostly from London. And here he built a school, and houses and a chapel, and made and administered the laws of a new society; so that, though we were born in the country, we were not countrymen, but members of a tiny self-supporting state of which grandfather was already the beneficent despot.

It was in '88 or '89 that my father and mother were married and grandfather moved out of the School House to make room for them, so that by the time I was able to bring my mind to bear upon him with any prospect of remembering, he had been living at the Farm nine or ten years. I saw him, therefore, established at the Farm; and for all any of us children knew he had inhabited it since the foundation of the world. There was always enough awe about our attitude towards him to make our visits to the Farm memorable. I do not name in particular any one occasion on which we were admitted to his court. On one of the twelve days of Christmas a children's tea-party was always held at the Farm, and we often went over to tea on Sundays.

It was a world of grown-ups, of aunts and uncles and visitors, all very strange and memorable, and its characteristic smell (every country house has its characteristic smell) was a smell of cakes in the cupboard. Their customs were then as different from ours as the customs of people in foreign countries are to-day. In our own family, father and mother sat side by side behind the tea-tray at the top of the table; in theirs, grandfather sat at one end and grandmother with her tea-urn at the other end of a very long table. It was with astonishment that we saw how differently grandfather drank his tea or ate his cake: we, in our manners, lifted the cup from the saucer, and left the saucer on the table; but grandfather lifted both together, and while he drank held the saucer in his left hand under the cup in his right. In our system, too, there were two distinct stages of food at tea—the prose or bread-and-butter stage, and the poetical or cake, bun and biscuit stage. We children ate our bread-and-butter dutifully so that we might eat our cake with delight. But grandfather would make a barbarous sandwich of a slice of cake between two slices of bread-and-butter, and eating this, would thus enjoy both kinds of provender at one bite. It was, I suppose, his own invention, and a king's prerogative; for I never saw anybody else try it. I shall never know now what practices distinguished him at other meals, for I never sat at any table with him but the tea-table. But long afterwards I heard it whispered (it has never been confirmed) that he drank beer at lunch time. I hope he did: we were brought up so strictly that the very name of beer was sin in our ears, but if this were true it could not damage grandfather's inviolable pedestal, and it could certainly lighten the burden on beer.

I must suppose that to-day is one of those Sundays when one or two of the older of us are invited to tea at the Farm. After the three o'clock service in the chapel, therefore, instead of hurrying back with our father to feed the cocks and hens in the school orchard, we are handed over to one or another of our aunts, and, holding tightly to her black gloves, and carrying her red-edged bible for her in the free hand, we walk in a little crowd past the alehouse and the cottages, by pond and barn, and turn in at the gate where the dark laurels and yews shade the gravelled drive. It is late summer, tea-time sunlight, with long cool shadows on the enclosed lawn, and a fire of sunset already reddening on the trunks of the Scots Pines. Tea is laid in the largest room at the Farm, on a long and crowded table. On the mantel-piece are grandmother's two glass lustres, all twink-ling in the window light, and the dozen prisms ready to swing and tinkle on their little swivels as soon as we ask Aunt Mary to touch them for us. In the farthest corner stands an ancient grand piano, and beside it a tall standing-lamp ready for the coming of darker evenings. Our relations all disappear to take off their hats and gloves; the elastic of our own sailor hats is withdrawn from our chins; Mr Larkin hangs his hat on one of the dozens of pegs in the passage, and greets us with a broad greeting and a rough hand under our chins. A tiny bell sounds; aunts pass through the hall from the kitchen to the tea-room with the tea-urn and the magic hot water jug that opens its own jaws as soon as grandmother tilts it to pour water. We are swept off by enormous black-frocked and black-coated adults to our places at the table. Carrie is forced to sit between Aunt Adelaide and Mr Larkin, and I am lifted into a chair (made more my size with a cushion) between Aunt Mary and Uncle Saul. Mr Larkin, I see, draws out his chair, gathers up his coat tails before he sits, and then draws in his chair again. Grandfather is at the north end of the long table, sitting bolt upright, his hands on his spread knees, the ghost of a royal smile playing above his beard. Without a word of warning, except the first note properly pitched by grandfather, the whole company (except me) breaks into song:

> Let us with a gladsome mind
> Praise the Lord, for he is kind;
> For his mercies shall endure,
> Ever faithful, ever sure.

Above the general company, grandfather's voice, with a genuinely gladsome sound, praises the Lord. To sing grace was not our own family way, and I never felt quite at ease about it. Our way was, at our father's signal, to shut our eyes and bow our heads over empty plates; and I remember a little uneasiness under the sung grace in my own heart, because we had not shut our eyes. It seemed too easy and novel a way, and I had my doubts about its efficacy. But God would understand, no doubt. Meanwhile, there they sat round about me—Mr Larkin, Aunt Mary, Aunt Adelaide, Uncle Saul,

Aunts Lydia and Bertha, grandfather, grandmother and all—lifting up their voices and opening their mouths. I was too awed to see the fun of it, except that Mr Larkin's brown beard wagged the words a little, and that grandfather would sing "Ever faithful, ever shoo-er."

Now tea began. Quince jam with the second slice, and by and by biscuits, and buns and cake, all of my grandmother's making, and tea to drink out of those enthralling blue and white cups which were so thin and delicately different from school crockery, and with the tiny, shiny blue medallions all embossed upon them, as apparent to touch as to sight. What the general conversation was, I now forget. Mr Larkin, no doubt, answered grandfather's talk about apples and hops by comparisons (in a broad Kentish brogue) with the apples and hops of Horseman-Den, where his farm lay. News had to be given and to be heard about the chapels of our neighbours, about London and the newspapers and the weather, and a hundred things of practical importance. But there was special aunts' talk for Carrie and me, carried on, as it were, from high to low level and amid the almost all-engrossing occupations of eating and choosing to eat. Grandfather meanwhile sandwiched his cake between slices of bread-and-butter, and drank, as you might say, more from midair than from the table level, and talked and laughed (but more generally nodded and smiled only) at the north. I looked up in the middle of the meal to notice that the heavy prisms of the lustres were still swinging from the touches of Aunt Mary. At the south end of the table, now that all the teacups had been filled from the urn, our grandmother sat silent. She wore a still and patient look. All the conversation missed her, for she was almost totally deaf. Suddenly something which Mr Larkin had said prompted grandfather to raise his voice and catch her eye across the whole length of the table. Whereupon she raised a black ear-trumpet from her lap, leaned forward fitting it to her ear, and listened while somebody loudly repeated the news into the trumpet for her delight. Her patience melted into smiles to show that she had heard; she nodded, and as she replaced the trumpet in her lap the smile slightly faded from her face. She went back into silence. Though social duty placed them at opposite ends of the table, grandfather never forgot her. He took pains to draw her into the conversation whenever he could. She seldom spoke, but when she did her voice was sweet and very soft. Most of her share in the talk was done by smiling; she had been deaf for many years.

When tea was done, and before the sunlight had

quite faded out, the whole party went into the garden, except those aunts who made it their duty to clear away the tea things. Even for the country the garden of the Farm was exceptional, a place to dream about, of quietness beyond description. Gowdhurst itself was forty miles out of London, a small and sleepy village; but the Farm was two further miles from this village, built on the crown of its own little hill, as I have told. It was a quiet neighbourhood on a Sunday. Even so, the Farm grounds were sanctuary from the neighbourhood. For trees rose out of a dense shrubbery of laurels and rhododendrons and berberis which quite enclosed the house and garden on its long eastern boundary. To the south, at the foot of the sloping lawn and garden, was a silent cobnut grove with larch trees, fruit trees and a hedge of holly to shut out the world; and to the west, beyond the old brick garden wall with its nectarines and ivy, and beyond the raspberries and gooseberries and a thick hedge of quick, the whole width of the cricket meadow lay between the house and the lane. All round this warded garden the land fell gently away to surrounding valleys, so that when we went out into the air after tea, and grandfather and Mr Larkin (with hands clasped under the tails of their frock-coats) paced up and down the lawn together, the only houses that they could see were more than two miles away upon the Gowd-hurst ridge, tiny models of houses peeping out for company among their fronded trees.

The lawn under the fir trees was mossy and golden, and scattered with fir-cones with which we delighted to play. Out in the open the lawn was covered with daisies and tiny yellow hawkbits. Here Carrie would play with me while all the grown-ups stood or sat about and talked. I can hear the stream oi their talk as I heard it then—an endless succession of words and words, such as grown-ups always use, a yes-my-dear and a no-my-dear kind of women's talk, as foreign to us as talk could be—and the occasional quiet laughs too from those groups where our uncles stood, and grandfather and Mr Larkin pacing the lawn near the flower border in talk as earnest as ever. It never entered my head then to criticize or object according to my own standards. It was a plain fact of existence that grown-ups lived their own lives and talked their own talk. It was not dull to me, either, because I did not try to understand it or avoid it; it was fact to be classed with the chatter of the water in a noisy corner of Combourne, or the sigh and hiss and roar of a wind all day; but it was quite as incomprehensible as either of these.

Carrie, being a girl, and four years older, found

more to interest her in their doings, and I was left alone with fir-cones and daddy-long-legs and daisies and worm-casts. Among so many enthralling little things I found myself busy at once. If in my coming and going I crossed the invisible path that my grandfather paced in company with his red-bearded friend, there would come out of the murmur of their conversation a sentence of friendliness for me. Grandfather would look at me across his philosophy, a very great distance, and smile far away, asking the world in general what Frank was doing now. But presently the sun went down indeed, and lamps were lit indoors. Then Aunt Lydia would laugh as she told me to come in with her; for the simplest practical statements always seemed to set her laughing; and they all went in together, climbing the high hearth-stoned front doorstep and stooping as they rubbed their shoes on the rough mat in the hall.

In the tea-room Uncle Bill was playing to himself (as you sing to yourself) on the tinkling grand piano in the corner. He lightly touched a gentle tune or two, pleasantly for its own sake, and stooped over the yellow keys. He gazed down between his knees at the floor, but as one hymn tune changed quietly into another, like the views of a dissolving lantern, so his attitude changed, and while he let his fingers wander on familiarly, he fixed his eye on a corner of the ceiling, as though there were a hole there through which he could see the violet sky above the fir tree tops. Nobody took the least notice of him. The music went softly on, filling the room as gently as the lamplight.

Before we settled down to the proper business of the evening, I persuaded Aunt Lydia to tinkle those lustre prisms again. My heart longed for one of the triangular rods of glass; I never saw them but I broke the commandment about coveting. They were each hung, by a chain of two faceted drops of glass, from a deep ruby-red glass stand. They were heavy, and ended in a spear-point, like the cut stopper of a vinegar bottle. They caught the lamplight un-expectedly and threw entrancing little bands of white and coloured light upon the white chimney-piece—bands which shivered and flickered when, as now, the finger of an aunt had set the prisms swinging.

Not very long afterwards it penetrated even to the Farm that lustres were old-fashioned and going out of favour, and when these were dismantled, oh joy of all first joys! somehow or other one of these prisms became mine, mine to have in and out of my pocket, to carry about with me, to feel the safe hard smooth sharpness of it in my hands, and, above all, to look through. To own such a crystal prism was to own a miracle, and I speak in sober maturity. All the miracles of this new century, its cars and gramophones and moving pictures in natural colour, are less than this prism was to me. For it was magic in essence, in its being and substance like a raindrop in a leaf. It was not a contrivance which could be made to do with wonderful ease something hitherto done with difficulty. No one had ever thought of the beauty of its natural operation, no one had invented it for any purpose or for none. It was as useless as the blue of the sky or the reflection of a pond-side tree, and it was pure and its beauty was startling and priceless. For a moment longer I must leave that company in the lamplit rooms of the Farm and tell about this lustre prism, because the opportunity may not arise again.

I forget the exact manner in which I got possession of it. Some aunt gave it to me when I begged for it, as no doubt I often did. Anyhow, there it was in my hand at last, six inches long, with three polished surfaces, a solid fragment of pure mathematics. I felt it heavy and cool, I felt up and down its three long smooth edges, its spear-point with a neck incurved. It was a fragment of harmonious space, the space that filled the sky, lying fixed in my palm. Then I laid one of its long facets across the bridge of my nose and looked in. The world was displaced, the horizon lay before my feet, the grass with its bright yellow stars sloped down and down, and I stood upon the verge of a strange earth, but an earth in which I saw again the coloured shadows of things familiar to me. And everything there—the sky, the branches of trees, the bright leaves and flowers, the rings and fingers of my aunt's hand—was edged with coloured fire, red and gold below, and above a blue and green and a deep and exciting violet. I went from person to person begging them to look at my new world, and then excitedly snatching the prism back again to my own eyes. I walked along precariously, for my feet were in one land and level and my eyes in another, and as I walked I could feel the downward world move up to meet me. It was my first taste of ecstasy, when present experience contradicts belief. The world was not the tame world to which I had grown accustomed, but this new unbalanced moving place, where all its commonest objects were transfigured by edges of godly colours; and yet it was the same old world. I loved this prism best when we went for our compulsory walk with Minnie Groves the nursemaid. Then in the lanes a little boy might be seen straggling along at the tail of a mail-cart, bent and intent upon something which nobody else could see, his eyes looking down into a long glass prism for minutes at a time, his feet stumbling along over the gritty road as though he walked in a dream.

I kept this treasure for years.

The proper business of the evening at the Farm had yet to be enjoyed. While the lustres were still swinging out their flashes, Aunt Lydia had drawn me to a chair, and had reached for the big scrap-book from the top of the piano. There together, while others less fortunate began to get dressed for the evening worship, she and I turned the heavy leaves of this ancient book. Everything was in it—everything, that is, which could be called a "scrap." No wonder if she found delight in it too, for it had been begun when she was a child, and she knew the proper stories to go with every page, as any author should, by heart. And round and about these queer chaotic prints went wreaths of embossed flowers, posies, ribbons, and silver bells. Each portrait of young beauties of the royal family, each view of the Great Exhibition, each review of the troops in red by the Queen in black, each saucy puppy or tangled kitten, each ogling beauty with gypsy locks, in artfully disarranged dress or stiff central European peasant costume, had its proper tale to go with it. The leaves were brown where fingers had turned them, some were getting worn and torn. But the scraps were not, they were as good as new. By and by as we turned we came to the page of all pages, which had two large scrap pictures mounted on it, the figures of two girls; and out of the mouth of one of them fell rings and diamonds and pearls, a heavy cascade of riches to her feet.

"Oh tell me this story!" said I, excitedly whispering.

"It must be the last to-night, then," said my aunt. "Once upon a time," she said, "there was a widow who had two daughters..." and so she told the whole story. But when she came to the pearls and diamonds of it, I had to go over the embossed scrap with my forefinger and count the words that had already fallen in jewels from the girl's lips. I knew them all and should have missed the least. At last, then, the story ended, and we were hatted and taken out into the dying day, across the meadow to school, to bed as soon as we had sung our hymns.

One day in the autumn of 1903 my grandfather drove himself home through pouring rain from Lamberhurst. He had driven through rain before, and had been till then too hearty and well to suffer for it. But he was seventy-three, and this time he took a serious chill. All that week-end we heard anxious grown-ups ask each other if he was better. On Saturday morning I went into school as usual, but before I went I asked the music-mistress as I met her how grandfather was to-day. She told me hastily that he was much better, and let me go on into school. There Beckett met me. "Have you heard about your grandfather?" he said. I answered as I had just been answered, that he was much better. But the music-mistress, kind heart, had lied to me, fearing, I suppose, to shock me with the truth, and Beckett told me that he was dead. I denied it, and I didn't believe him. Neither he nor I knew what death meant, it was no more than a word to us; but I thought and thought, and by the behaviour of others to me, and by strange goings on out of all time-tables, I concluded that Beckett was right. But I did not know, I could not imagine what grandfather's dying could mean. He was as a sun in the little world we knew, and I could not see a world at all without him.

When we came out from school I found my mother and Miss Richardson at the sewing machines, making crêpe bands for the boys to wear on their arms. I felt that the world was raw and uneasy and inexplicably changing, but I was not really sad about it at all, nor do I remember noticing the sadness of other people much.

On the morning of the funeral day many of the boys were taken across to the Farm to see him lying in his coffin. I did not go then; but presently my father came to me, and took me over to the Farm with him alone. Many wreaths filled the house there with a strange and suffocating scent. Grandfather's coffin was in the room on the left; it was of yellow wood, and stood on low trestles. My father held my hand while we went in together; he was pale and his head was bent. For a minute or two he said nothing to me; but at last, gently taking my right hand, he whispered to me to touch grandfather's face and feel how cold he was. I did as he asked me, but I could not weep. I only knew that my father was different.

By novelty after novelty, by the scent of lilies, the black bands on our arms, the whispering of people, the drawn blinds and the twilight of the rooms near the road, weight of the strangeness of death collected upon me. I was taken to the funeral service in the chapel where he had preached, and saw again, but with a shock to find it closed now, the heavy coffin where I had seen him in the morning. They sang a hymn or two, of which somehow or other the slow weeping music of "Peace, perfect Peace" struck a deadly horror into my heart. And then, while all the rest of the school and household walked or rode the two miles to the village cemetery, I was taken back to the school.

It was silent and empty, as if to-day were the first day of holidays, only the blinds were still drawn. I felt a kind of coldness and was puzzled by it, but before the mourners were back again, and life had begun to resume old courses, I had let my puzzling go. I found a book of rhymes and pictures (I can see the page again now and the big straggling verses and pictures of the House that Jack Built). I do not remember crying once. I did not know that he was dead.

10

The "X"

OUR life, I see now, was one long festival, and
its programme was the programme of the
seasons. We were a large family, the lower
end of which, as it constantly renewed itself, ab-
sorbed most of the adult attention which might
otherwise have been bestowed upon us, and we
lived at a school, where our parents were content
to know that children mostly come to no harm if
they are left to themselves. We were lucky in being
left to ourselves. Ponds, hayfields, orchards and
woods were ours without need of passport; we had
gardens of our own, and, when the time came, John
and I had a workshop of our own where we would
spend the whole length of summer daylight happily,
and not be willing, even then, to go to bed at the
legal time at night. In all our long childhood we
were never willingly idle. By comparison with our
own intoxicating occupations of the day, school
itself seemed a kind of idleness, and we lived then
for the dismisses (as we called the breaks between
classwork) and for the Saturday half holidays. There
was no tyranny in our large family, and a great deal

of wholesome independence. When lead-casting was my vocation, rat-hunting by catapult was John's; while I was inventing the mechanism of crossbows, John was making "Home Sweet Home" in fretwork on a red plush background. But when the summer holidays came, there were three passions which we always shared: lazy daylong fishing in the ponds, the making of bows and arrows (real, deadly weapons, constructed out of well-chosen and shaped staves cut by ourselves from Our Wood), and that richest of all summer delights, bathing and raft-making—dabbling all day in wetness.

Early in every summer term the occasion of a traditional school festival, called by us the X, mildly inaugurated fishing. On this holiday certain of the older boys were allowed to construct elaborately decorated fishponds, and the first thing, as anyone may know, is to catch fish. Now the manner of a fishpond is this: It is constructed in the covered-playground in a space allotted to you; you beg and borrow a zinc bath, or a butt or a barrel cut in half; if it leaks you caulk it with clay and pitch till it will hold water. About this barrel you build an arbour with long boughs of summer trees, and moss and flowers, so as to disguise your barrel into a pond, and on the pond you may float lilies and their leaves, and if your soul is in science you may devise a fountain in the pool, or a waterfall that turns a little mill. But above all you must have fish in your pond, and boughs above it.

It was astonishing how soon twenty or thirty boys, competing, could quite transform the dark and dusty covered-playground into a moist, leafy, tinkling forest. The sweet smells of weeds out of the water and of bruised leaves pervaded that side of the school all day. The fishponds were legal only on the very day of the X. They must be complete by noon, too; which made it necessary for any competitor to rise, that day, as early as he could wake. At noon the judges went round and awarded prizes; by bed-time the arbours had to be denuded and the fishponds empty. A week before the day a few of the more enterprising boys went down to the ponds to fish. Two days before the day, wash-basins and water-cans and jars (but all illegally appropriated) were fetched to hold the fish. Many died; a few were bought and sold.

We children of six-to-eight went, not to school proper with its big classes and long, echoing passages, but to a little kindergarten school held in a room at the back of the chapel. There must have been five or six pupils at that time learning their letters. Our classroom had no desks or forms. It had a table where Miss Bee sat, a blackboard on an easel, and a cupboard which was kept locked. Built in at the back of the room was a giant wooden staircase of only three or four steps rising from the floor, and we sat on these stairs to be instructed. We wrote our letters and did our sums on slates, and our slate pencils were sharpened every morning on the stone doorstep by the monitor for the week. This *monitor* was one of us, boy or girl, appointed to bear responsibility. He collected the slates and gave them out again, he helped Miss Bee to tidy her sacred cupboard, where chalk and dusters and reading-books and a globe were stored away. He sharpened pencils and cleaned the blackboard. Every day the duster was wetted and the board made black and spotless. When I was monitor I was sent out, according to routine, to wet the duster in the rain-water butt by the side of the headmaster's house. On this side of the house grew two large cherry trees, and a ladder lay up to the branches of the further tree, for it was July when cherries are ripe and rain is scarce. The water in the butt was so low and I was so short in my legs, that with all my efforts I was unable to get the duster under the water. I reached over the sides of the butt again; I made a grand effort and, tipping forward, slid head downwards into the water. And there I should have drowned, had not Miss Bee's sister seen me from the top of the ladder, where she was picking cherries. I struggled and kicked, but I could not cry out, because I was under the water. She rushed down from the ladder, dropping her basket of cherries, and pulled me out in time. I cried and coughed and was taken back to bed, and did no more school that day. This happened a week or so before the X.

Hugh Harvey, who was two years my senior, had lately been moved from our kindergarten to the big school, and we envied him the privileges which he was enjoying there. Towards the end of July came the great X day. "To-morrow is the X," we all said with excited eyes. But we were compelled to toil away in our little dark classroom, far from all the stir and preparation. School gardens were being weeded and watered through every dismiss, and we could not help or look on. Fish were being caught and fishponds selected. Hugh could see these things just outside his classroom door; we could see, from our classroom window, nothing but the domed top of a weeping-ash tree and half a dozen pines from whose cones through the hot day winged seeds came spinning down drunkenly, past the window and across the brilliant sky.

After breakfast on the morning of the great day, and before we were taken down to school, we had peeped into the dark covered-playground. Already the tree boughs were being brought in, their dark dry green scent filled our nostrils, there was a noise of water being poured into tubs, pond-water that smelt of duck-weed, white waterlilies and living fishes. The place was in the chaos of preparation, hammering and sawing and chopping of wood went on. Boys continually darkened the whole double playground doors with the boughs they were fetching—and from this enticing scene we were taken away to school, where we sat indoors while the sun scorched the fir-cones open above our roof, where we stayed indoors squeaking thoughtlessly on our slates, unable to make a good pothook, or get a simple addition sum done rightly, because our hearts were with the fishponds.

But at half past eleven we all ran out to play. We were at that time permitted to run about the grass in the chapel yard under the fir trees and the weeping-ash, beside the graves of George Vousden and George Allcorn, the only two of my grandfather's flock who were buried near their church. On other days I should have been content to stay there with the rest, collecting cones and dandelions, or staring through the hedge at Mr Bee's chickens. Ten minutes of play was allowed, and then by some signal Miss Bee would be calling us back to work till half past twelve and dinner-time. But to-day I could not stop there. When no one was looking I turned from the place, stole out of the gates safely and into the road. I meant no more than a short run to the playground gate, a peep to see how many fishponds were ready, and then I would run back again in easy time to go on with unwelcome work. The short road was long and dusty to my guilty feet. I reached the playground gate; I peeped in, into the green, wet, scented darkness and bustle. Things had gone on even better than I had imagined. My heart, though heavy with a new sin, still kept me there. Back to school I never went, but I presented myself, with what innocence I could muster, at the dinner-table promptly. And there I found that I had sisters to defeat me. My absence had, of course, been reported. People had been looking for me, wondering if I had really managed to drown myself at last; and when the whole story came out, it came with my bitter tears. I was not punished that time, but badly rebuked, and then hurried off to be crammed into my white shorts and sailor blouse, to make me fit to watch in the blazing sun while the boys of the big school went through their drills and their stretcher practices.

Afterwards we looked at the fishponds by right; we touched the golden backs of translucent carp and roach and minnows, and saw them shoot away, laziness even in a hurry, to the dark shadows in the tub; we saw the water lily's light, and her broad floating leaves, and heard all the waterfalls and fountains of the scientific. Thus I first saw fishes alive.

After the X, the term slipped rapidly away, and holidays began with August, when glow-worms shone in the evenings, and early apples were ripe, and hay was cut and carted. At once one or two of the older boys, of those who generally stayed at school during the holidays, spent all their pocket money in rods and lines, searched for wasps' nests and raided them for gentles to use as bait, and settled down seriously to fishing. On the school grounds there were six ponds: the Flood, the Bathing Pond, the Cricket Pond, Three-Ponds, the Little Pond, and one, without any distinguishing name at all, which was deep and prolific, and lay in a hollow just behind the playground and the slope we called Mount Sinai. All round this pond were the flat-topped stumps of felled trees, and down the steep sides bushes of blackberry and hawthorn grew over the water. The water was very dark and deep, but a few reeds grew at one end where the fall was most gradual. The north side of the pond was covered in with a thick growth of sapling oaks and maples, whose boughs grew out low over the water, and afforded foothold for those who wished to fish in the deepest parts. Our favourite point was, however, on the south side, where an oak stump like a round table-top jutted out over the perpendicular bank, so that you looked over its edge through four feet of air into eight feet of brown water lying quiet in a bay between two of the bramble bushes. Here John and I would sit, when we were very young, by the side of boys big enough to hold the long ash rod they had cut, and watch the whole process and art of pond fishing. We knew how to fish before we ever touched a rod.

At last we grew old enough to have ash rods of our own; at last we were allowed to buy lines with particoloured bobfloats and hooks and gut and sinkers, and to go fishing alone. I see us now, from the playground stile: two urchins aged nine and eleven, with indigo jerseys buttoned on the shoulder, and serge shorts, and unevenly rolled stockings, marching together across the hay stubble towards Three-Ponds, the deepest of all. Our rather crooked rods, with their new lines twisted round them, we carried at the slope; bait was in our pockets, bait made with moist bread and treacle; and in our hands a glass jar each in which to put the little fishes.

It was the middle of August, the end of a hot

summer. From Steeven's cornfields on the other slope we could hear the rattle of a reaping machine, and we could see, too, the nodding horses, far away but clear above the wood, and the labourers stooping to bind the corn in the armfuls that they gathered up from the straight row of fallen corn behind the reaper. A haze of grey heat lay over the Gowdhurst hillside, all the bright fields were getting golden, and all the shadows purple and uncertain. There was no noise at all of sheep or cattle or birds, or any animal; but a vast hum of insects—bees, dragonflies and grasshoppers—which stirred about our feet as we kicked along through the stubble over the dry, cracked meadows.

To fish in Three-Ponds was an adventure in itself. The pond behind the school, though probably richer in fishes, was too near to civil life; a bell would ring for us to go to tea, and if we still dallied there, a maid could come down from the kitchen to the laurels at the top of the opposite bank and call us home. But Three-Ponds was half-a-mile away across fields, and buried there in its own nut trees and brambles; Three-Ponds was silent and deep and mysterious, quite shut away from laws of time and hunger and (if truth be told) really forbidden. Its nuts were sweet and within our fourfoot reach; its blackberries, too, were excellent; but its depth was a danger with which (with precautions) we really loved to flatter ourselves. Altogether it was an attractive place, and we two were going there this afternoon, according to our fancies with stealthy tread.

The hay stubble was dry and crackly; we passed the Little Pond, where tench had once been caught; we passed, too, the Bathing Pond with its terraced banks of grass and clay; we crossed into the last field, the football field in winter, and, ducking under the screens of hawthorn and hazel, stooped along the dark steep path through woods to the edge of the water, which opened out suddenly from the bank, and lay there asleep in the hot afternoon glare. Its silence, its entire freedom from the taint of humanity, gave Three-Ponds a positive presence. You did not speak quite in your own voice there, but hushed your spirit in awe of its reputed depth, and looked across the lily leaves into a kind of eternity. Here we settled down to fishing.

We unrolled our lines, and set the bobfloat high for deep water, because carp, which were our hope, hang about in deep places. We solemnly baited our hooks together, and having arrived at an agreement about territorial waters, cast out and sat down to wait. Each boy fixed his gaze upon his own float. Little tremors and bobbings of the float made wrinkles on the smooth water; from the open end of the pond a wind cut in and drove arrow heads of wavelets across the clear spaces between the lilies. Our floats were still again. Behind us, over our heads, all about us, the burning sun was at its work, drying the black broom pods. Every now and again we heard one crackle and snap its springy sides suddenly, catapulting its round brown seeds into the air. We heard them patter on the leaves and fall with a tiny splash into the water. Giant dragonflies with eyes like melting jewels darted at the tips of our fishing rods, or settled quiveringly upon the edges of the lily-leaves; and as they flew here and there, hunting for smaller insects, we could hear the papery rustle of their wings. Great bumble-bees, too, came booming in from the dry fields in search of any late flower by the pond, and ten million flying things unseen— midges and bluebottles, wasps and hover flies—kept up a murmur so constant and so characteristic of the afternoon that it sounded to us like the silence of the sleeping heat.

"Krig-krig!" said a moorhen away in a creek.

"You've got a bite," said John in a whisper.

Our floats had drifted nearer together, and now mine was the source of many little circles of waves. It dipped and danced, so that I could hardly bear to wait (as I knew one should) for the complete sub-merging of the cork. John's coloured buoy bobbed on the wavelets which mine awakened, and at last I thought it was time to pull in. I snatched the wet cord from the water. The bait was gone from the hook, but "I felt him," I cried, "I felt him! A whopper!" and baited again in haste.

Meanwhile John's float began to dance on its own account, and I waited, therefore, and did not cast out my line again. After a succession of nibbles and dances John's float suddenly became alive, and plunged with purpose forward and down under the water. I saw his line go taut as he stood up. The fish, which was certainly a prize, was hooked.

John did not play him out, for our pond-fishing was downright pull and catch, with none of the refinements of fly-fishing. He hauled in with diffi-culty a carp, as I swear, the largest ever seen. John swung him heavily on to the bank, where he beat the dry turf loudly with his tense body, and he would surely have been in the water again had I not flung down my tackle with a careless splash, and gone for him on hands and knees. I can feel him yet as hard as metal and as slippery as a piece of soap, tightening his springy muscles under my fingers and dancing in the dust. His great eyes stuck out from his head like gold-rimmed stones, his parchment gill-covers opened and shut, his thick white lips emitted silent shouts of fear.

"I've got him!" I sang, though it was all that I could do to keep him in my two hands.

"Hold him, hold him!" sang John.

That fish took more than half an hour to die, and during the whole time we watched him together. At first he grew weaker quickly, and his struggles seemed to be coming to a safe end, only his mouth and red-edged gills kept moving for the water he desired so. Then John laid him in a safe place beside a root of couch grass. But when we turned back to our lines a fresh paroxysm seized him, his body bent again and unbent like a bow, he leapt upon his side, and tried to slip past our four hands to the pond again. So John went on holding him, and I went on admiring him, till his gasping died again to a gentle flicker of the gills, and then we knew that he was safely dead.

I must confess that we felt no sympathy then; and I think that most of our callousness was due to the dumbness of fishes. Long afterwards when I was taken out by a Frenchman to catch edible frogs, their pitiable screaming when they were hooked made me hate the sport; but a fish is dumb and limbless, and you do not gather from him how much or how little he is hurt. Certainly I remember disliking the necessary task of wrenching the barbed hook out of cartilaginous lips, and even more the evil and bloody process (which Reggie and some others of the older boys practised) of stunning a fish by battering its head with a knife-handle or a stone; but this dislike was due to my own disgust more than to any pain which I might suppose the fish suffered. And when we went to fish in the company of Carrie or Stella we would make a great bravado of our comparative courage, and coolly unhook for them what fishes they caught. What pleasure girls found in fishing was a question to us: their excitement at a catch was more than half fear, yet though they pretended to hate touching and unhooking their fishes, they would sit again for a long half hour, only to shudder when they succeeded in doing what, after all, they had come out on purpose to do. We were not so tender-hearted.

"He's big enough to eat," I said to John.

John nodded; he was pardonably proud.

"I shall get Caroline to cook him for my breakfast," he said.

So we fished through the rest of the long hot afternoon, and neither of us caught another fish.

As daily occupation for small boys such pond-fishing was very inadequate. Its novelty, and the alluring fact that what was forbidden in term was allowed in holidays, attracted us to it at the beginning of every summer holiday; but a week's freedom to fish exhausted our interest. Then it was that we turned to bows and arrows. These too, as being dangerous, were forbidden during term, so that it would have been a duty in any case to devote some time to them, if only to assure ourselves of the freedom that we enjoyed. We began with rough garden sticks, and thought a thirty yard shot a good thing. We ended by each championing his own kind of wood against all others, and our bows were more dangerous than a toy should be.

It took a day, almost, to make a bow as we finally made it. We cut a pole and peeled it, and then with a spoke-shave tapered it from the hold to each end. But the green wood was tough, and the spoke-shave was blunt, and we were only small. The floor of our workshop, by the time we had finished, was covered with the scented strippings, and we finished the wood to smoothness with the edges of broken glass. Hazel wood had for a long time been most favoured. For one thing, in copses, hazel quickly grew long straight poles, more quickly than ash or chestnut; chestnut when young was too sodden and green, and ash too brittle; hazel had long fibres and did not snap across the grain; its only fault was that, as we used it straight from the tree, it very soon lost its spring.

Down in the wood I was, alone, I remember, cutting long sucker shoots for arrows, and I was far away, beyond the spring, at the crab-apple end of the wood. There in my wanderings I saw a long straight slender corky maple bough, and took note of it, and wondered how maple wood would behave as a bow. John and I, at that time, had excellent bows of hazel, of which we were boastful; and competition (at least in my ideas) was keen; when my bow broke and I remembered the maple. I cut it with the meat saw (which I borrowed out of the kitchen) and set it on our bench at once to shave off the ridges of cork. It was a dry slow-grown piece of wood, and I took the very greatest care with it, and shaped it that day, but too late to string it.

Next morning I strung it with whipcord, a newly bought piece, and twanged it and thought it was good. But before I shot its first arrow I found that I was out of the fashion, John and a friend of his called Spencer had suddenly transferred all interest from bows and arrows, which were just legal, to the far more deadly and quite illegal catapult. They could think about nothing else that morning, and were off to shoot at water rats down Three-Ponds way, while I was choosing the longest straightest wire-bound arrow to try in my maple bow. So I took a little trial shot, up into the apple boughs outside the workshop door, and then, collecting the arrow, went up to the lawn this side of the damson trees, and shot that arrow with grace and ease to a distance never equalled. I shot it, as I said, from the lawn, over the damson trees and the kitchen garden, over the highest roof of the school and the elm trees beyond so that it fell into the Farm orchard that lay on the other side of the road, opposite the nursery window. Nobody was there to see my triumph; nobody but I saw the sure way that the arrow mounted as it left the bow, singing. Nobody else saw it rise as though it would kiss the sky, and then begin to curve and fall and swing, high over the ridge of the roof, high up over the flagstaff even, and shoot past downwards out of sight behind the dark-leaved elms.

11

Tunbridge Wells Adventures

THE musical uncle, Uncle Bill, kept a dairy in Tunbridge Wells. His shop had the clean, hard, cold nature of dairies, the window had in it china swans, with their wings up and their backs full of eggs, and clear jars of honey, as well as honey in the comb, and model milk churns daily polished, models still, but oh, much nearer to reality than that silver milk churn of my grandmother's. His name stood over his shop. It was a pleasant shock to modesty to see it there, for it was my name too, and I fancied that every one passing read it, from the coalmen clip-clopping by on their wagons, to the smart gentlemen in spectacles who sat in the caves of hansoms with the apron shut over their legs, and looked as though they intended to see nothing but what was still far ahead. But they saw that name, no doubt, and me standing there gazing up at it; for to me it was the most important name in the world.

But while I have been gazing up at it—I, a boy of six or so—the traffic of Calverley Road has been streaming by: ladies in fashions incredibly hideous, blown balloon sleeves, collars almost to the ears, spindle-waists, and forward-tilted straw hats, have been pattering by to the jeweller's or the grocer's, or to Witson's next door, the best butcher of the town, or to buy stamps from little Miss Batterbee in the Post Office over the way; and gentlemen, too, in tall hats and very long starch-enclosed necks, or gentlemen with weeping moustaches and cloth caps; all of whom seemed perfectly normal inhabitants of the Wells, and aroused no wonder or aversion in my heart. Not a cigarette to be seen there, not a felt hat, not a car, not an ankle or a knee—and all clothes safe and sombre and rather thick and slow.

I am staying, you see, with Uncle Bill, in 1899. One of his sisters keeps house for him in a tiny house at the back of the dairy. I did not know she was his sister, but only that she was my aunt, for I had never thought much about the relationships of people, except as relative to me. This was Aunt Bertha, the duchess, whom I really liked best of all because of her soft voice and imperturbable way of smiling. She served in the dairy too, and smiled across the marble counter on all her customers— that is to say, she had a look of quietness out of which she smiled at you, but not to part her lips. I thought she was very beautiful; her hair was fair and cloudy, and she never raised her voice or wanted things done in a hurry.

You climbed from the tiles of the dairy floor up five stone steps to the door into the house. This led into the room where you sat down to ordinary tea. A fire was in the other corner, and a tiny shelf by the window. The window did not, like most windows, look out at the sky, but into a stone-flagged scullery, and this had no windows at all, but a sloping glass roof. A separator stood in a dark corner there, and a marvellous serpent of water pipes used for cooling the milk. Through the chinks of the wooden wall (for the scullery was really only a yard with a roof) a warm, raw smell came in, and subdued lowings and bleatings now and then, and scuffles and thuds, from Mr Witson's slaughter-house. My aunt and uncle kept a wise silence about these goings on, and I did not know then that beasts were put to death within a few feet of where I stood. Charlie's stable was in the passage outside, and there I was shown the slings, still in position, where he had hung suspended by doctor's orders after a fall in frosty weather. I liked the stable.

Aunt Bertha took me round and told me about things. It was a queer cramped, tight, airless little house, but I did not mind that so much, because it was full of novelties. That strange smell of singeing, for instance, which hung about in the passage between dairy and scullery, came from an operation which I delighted to watch. Uncle Bill was there in apron and cap, preparing poultry for sale. I did not see the early processes of plucking and drawing the fowls, but here at this slab he took the limp, naked birds in hand. He cut off their heads, and trussed their legs and wings with wooden skewers, clipping off the spare ends of the skewers with snips, and patting the plump, pale bodies into shape. Then and there at a gas flame he rapidly singed the whole of the bodies, brushed them, and floured them and set them side by side upon a tray, having artfully changed them, in this process, from limp, repellent corpses to plump and attractive articles of merchandise. Meanwhile I collected the clipped ends of skewers into match-boxes—nice round little rods of white wood. They were quite useless, yet they seemed too neat and uniform to be left wasting there.

Just by the slab where the fowls were singed and trussed was a low, dark door. It did not lead into any room or passage, like common doors, but, opening inwards, swung out high above stone steps, which led down into a dungeon deep under ground. It was all hollow and dark, dark as night of course, even in the day-time; but, by a magical switch at the entrance, even my finger, reaching up, could flood its damp deeps with electric light; and in this cellar anyone might hear the echoes of a loud slapping noise, where another aunt (my mother's youngest sister and really no more than a girl) made up those neat rectangular and circular pounds and halves of butter every day, and stamped them with the image of a dairy swan before she folded them up in crackling wet paper. This was Aunt Vye, noted for this remarkable subterranean work; she had planted a holly berry and a lemon pip in pots which stood on the little window shelf in the tea-room, where both of them grew and flourished; also Miss Batterbee was her special friend. There was nothing remarkable about Miss Batterbee except her name. It struck me as a good, strange, laughable, Yorkshire-pudding sort of name, and I played with it at night, after the electric light was switched off, and mixed it up with the other phenomena of living in a town: the light of street lamps on your bedroom walls, and the noise of people going by so late that they were still going by, and their stony steps echoing and their infrequent voices receding, when you were on the edge of sleep.

On Sunday we took tea upstairs (which was one wonder) by the side of a gas-fire (which was another). To take tea upstairs was, to anyone of normal country habits, a beautiful reversal. In common country life one went upstairs to bed, but came downstairs to eat. How incredible, I thought—as I gazed out of the window down on the heads of passers-by—how incredible it is that here I am upstairs and yet, in a turn of the head, there is the drawing-room, a downstairs room, and the tea-table, a downstairs table. All the while that I sat at tea I felt this elevation, and ate my bread-and-butter and my biscuits differently, in a first floor hush. And the gas-fire was a natural wonder; like the burning bush in the Bible, it burned and was not consumed. I liked everything at "The Dairy," the cold shop with its buttery smell, the little dark rooms, the ominous cellar, the tea upstairs, the lying awake at night by the light of street lamps which nobody felt it their duty to put out; but all these things I might have forgotten had not two incidents helped to fix the place for ever in my mind.

The setting for each is a quiet town by night, but there they fall apart; for the first is hardly to be called an event at all, and the second is all-eventful, and remembered, no doubt, by hundreds of residents of the town. The first is a walk I took; the second is a torchlight procession.

I had been at the Dairy a week, I suppose, and now that the electric light and shop life were beginning to lose their novelty, I sometimes thought, with a tiny inexplicable ache, of home again. One night Uncle Bill proposed a walk, and we set out together, hand in hand, under the branches of light of the street lamp trees. It was a cold night, a shadowy night, with a very black starless sky overhead, and very dazzling rows of street lamps before us. Every now and again a solitary figure of man or woman, whose steps we had heard ringing before us, detached itself from the shadows and walked through the light towards us and past us. We went through streets that had no shops at all, on and on into what was obviously a hopelessly dark world. Presently we mounted to a corner of the pavement where the street ran up into a main road, long and straight, and running away from us, with its lamps among tree boughs, to our right and left. We stopped on the corner and stood together looking down the long vista to the left. There was a light mist on the air, enough to emphasize the unreality of the gaslight, and the length and distance of the far road.

"That's the way home," said Uncle Bill.

Puzzled by a choking in my chest, I peered down and down under the lamps and trees; and they and the road did not end, but died and dissolved on the night. "Is it very far?" I asked him.

"About twelve miles," said he, with careless

ease. A monstrous distance! Hop-o'-my-Thumb came into my mind: how his mother and father led them out into the wood, far away from familiar paths, on purpose to lose them; and how they came back once and twice, but were lost the third time, and how Hop-o'-my-Thumb climbed a tree at night, and spied a light far off. There I stopped considering the tale; it was a sense of the vastness of the world—a feeling of being lost, and calling down long echoing avenues—that suddenly overcame me. I held tighter to my uncle's hand when I asked: "Is it very far?" Oh, it seemed an untraversed desert of twelve miles, with darkness to walk into, and no hope at all of ever finding one's way home.

But we turned back again under the light-enchanted trees, and came in by the back door (for the shop door was closed), and I went to bed. Sleep soon comforted me, and the morning came, the morning of the day whose evening was to witness wonders like living fairy tales. For I had been promised the torchlight procession, and my imagination already painted it vividly. I did my best to get through the day, but it seemed longer than other days. I ran over gladly with a message or two to Miss Batterbee; I collected several matchboxfuls of skewer ends; I went down into the cellar and saw the bowl of water where the wooden pats, and the wooden mould of the swan upside down, were kept wet for their work, and at last tea-time came, and lamplight, and, after tea, time to go out into the night.

Surely all four of us went together that evening— yet now I remember it, vividly and clearly, with only two in the adventure: my aunt, whose hand I held, and myself. Aunt Vye, I suppose, had gone with her friend Miss Batterbee, and Uncle Bill, perhaps, was kept at home by trade and duty.

The streets were thronged with people as if in a dream. We walked until we came, by a sudden turn, full in front of the iron gateway of a park. The crowd was thicker here; no doubt a larger crowd than I had ever seen, if I had thought to notice it; but I remember nothing at all of all the shadowy people, only these gates into a park, and beyond them, gemming the night, thousands of fairy lamps in ropes and chains and long festoons, lining the gravelled walks, and swinging across from tree to tree among the very leaves, twinkling in every colour, dancing, too, with the dancing of the twigs from which they hung, brighter than stars or any natural light whatever, and lovelier in their coloured novelty than day or starlight. I was lifted quite out of speech by the sight, so that tears began to collect in my eyes as we approached the gates, tears which half dissolved the fairy lights and made long tram-beams.

If I had been alone I should never have entered the park; but the strange grown-up, who held me by the hand, walked on with normal pace, and we bought tickets under the spitting light of an arc lamp by the gate, and moved on down the gravel till we were actually within touching distance of the loops of lamps that lined the drive. There we went in, and walked upon the wet grasses unmolested, while groups of dark laughers came and went, and from not far the blown-about music of an orchestra saluted my ears. But all was one, that night, all crowds and their excitement, all wind-borne music, all the heavy roof of night in whose magic recesses and caves we wandered, one joy in my soul, and only to be expressed (as though by symbol) by the liquid brilliant dangerous lights among the leaves. I cannot remember a single simple happening—only all the night is now in the picture of a wide-branching tree, with its trunk softly lighted by the paper lanterns hung under its arbours, and the tangled lamps (Aladdin's glassy fruits), shining yellow and red and deep pure blue, everywhere among its twigs. The band is in this picture and the dark impersonal presence of a moving crowd, and grass underfoot surprised by this nether day into an underwater greenness. I found nothing common to remember there, not even the passing of Time, and came away in the same dream as overtook me at our entry, returned to dark streets, and useful lamps on tall standards.

We did not return to the Dairy at once, but entered some strange house on the side of Mount Pleasant, and were chucked under chin by gentlemen who thought to banish, by this familiarity, the shyness that is due to strangers. So we climbed the stairs, everything strange and with a different smell, until we came to a high bedroom, where the window was up, and Miss Batterbee half in and half out in the night. Up through the air and in at the window the usual street noises came clearly to us. Our bodies filled the window, my head and shoulders between the plumper bodies of Miss Batterbee and my aunt. They chattered on, and found the waiting dull. I found it dizzy. I was not yet quite out of my dream of the coloured lights, and I had never felt so high above the earth; I felt the very weight of the dark immeasurable space upon me, and looked down upon the tiny street lamps and the dim figures of moving and collecting crowds. We waited ten exciting minutes, and then the sound of music rolled up the gigantic passage of Mount Pleasant, and my aunt's "here they come" was but an elevated expression in words of the turning expectation that was visible along the banks of human heads below. Then round the corner by the station bridge appeared the red and smoky glare of torches, and I heard the music suddenly burst into the astounded street, and the tramp-tramp of the feet, and the emphatic and ominous drums.

Noise and light intensified, cheers began to rise from the crowds on each pavement, the head of the human snake came up with us, the long body, lined with flaring torches, wound on and on below us. Every one was shouting, singing the song that the band was playing. I heard Miss Batterbee's surprising treble above my head, and whether I knew the words then or not, these, I know, are something like her words:

When you've finished Rule Britannia,
When you've sung "God save the Queen,"
When you've finished killing Krüger with your mouth,
Will you kindly drop a shilling
In my little tambourine,
For the gentlemen in Khaki ordered south:
Cook's son, Duke's son, son of a millionaire,
Forty thousand horse and foot going to Table Bay,
Each of 'em doing his country's work, but who's to look after
the kids?
So pass the hat for your credit's sake
and Pay, pay, pay!

All was remote and objective, till I was suddenly aware of two warm pennies being thrust into my hand, and some unintelligible instructions being given to me at the same time. I sang all I knew, which was Pay, pay, pay! Along the edges of the snake of Khaki many little figures were dodging to and fro in front of the crowd. These were clowns, they carried tambourines and collected money. But soon afterwards came the kings of the clowns, men with hideously patterned faces of black and white and red, who carried canvas bags on the ends of long bamboos and danced them under the noses of the window-spectators. I dropped my pence into one of these proffered bags; and soon afterwards the crowd turned into the road below, filling it up as the procession passed on, and went streaming off; while the music (all but the heart-penetrating thuds of those big drums) died away towards Monson Road. So we three drew in our heads and shut the window, and as we came downstairs every grown-up that met us asked me if I had liked it. I nodded my ginger head at them, and went on and on with my aunt, out into the street, home to the dairy. The next day I was driven home to Gowdhurst, and I thought, as I went, of bands and soldiers and the delights of war-time. In my pocket I carried home a match-box full of skewer ends, and in my head a tale of a night transformed which (now that I have tried) I know is beyond telling.

12

Birds and Flowers

Now it is time for me to try to tell about the birds and animals and flowers of this early land. Conceive this world, its littleness and its vastness, hill after hill, valley after valley, clothed with trees, as I began to describe it at the beginning of the book; and the great cap of the sky, the night sky and the day sky, eyed with stars or made friendlier by clouds; the sun in it above the winter-solid hills of earth. And then all the little things, whose vastness was their number and variety: a flock of starlings blackening a field in February; rooks wheeling and calling in the wind above the bare elms; a lonely heron, one long-legged spot in an empty sky; and the carpet of the fields in May, when any glance included thousands of lives of colour and joy, and one could only escape in sleep from the rapids of lives. Mice in all the woods and hedges, moles in every field, birds in every bush and gable, snakes in the grass, flowers in the grass, bees and butterflies and spiders by their millions in the flowers, midges in the wind, fishes in the ponds, wasps in the summer banks, glow-worms at night, snails and slugs and caterpillars, ladybirds, dragon-flies, cockchafers, jays, jackdaws, hawks, wrens, blue-tits, chaffinches, tomtits, robins by the thousand, sparrows for ever, and a cuckoo by day and a nightingale by night. The individuals, the creatures, in their numbers were inexhaustible, and each one full of his own life, the axis of a world, escaping and fleeing death; ants plotting against adversity, main-taining that an ant-hill is the centre of the universe; birds eating ants that a bird may survive—and into this hive of life *we* were born, thinking nothing about our own limitations, but given a sense of wonder and eyes to watch, and left thus to our own devices to get what joy the appearances of life might afford us.

This, it is true, is a later sight of it: it comes after the exercise of that distinctively grown-up power of detaching oneself from the world surreptitiously, and watching while the vast confusing play goes on unsuspecting. But in those days we were as much creatures of the earth as any bird whose conscious-ness I cannot pretend detaches it from the world. We were worldlings too. The spring came from the earth into us, the riot of summer also troubled our blood, and in all we were the creatures' brothers. We, too, were straws in the long currents of life, and our happiness was as self-kindling as the lark's, and, like the lark, we hardly knew we sang. Only we were different in this: that we had no hunting to do, and had leisure therefore to learn to observe, when the creatures had none; for our nurture was provided for us, and dinner-time seemed as much a plan of the world about us as morning or evening. Yet even in this we were not much divided from the creatures, for we were young, like lambs, and rightly expected our food, and those who were our elders (like sheep, I almost said) rightly gave it to us. Nature was not our background, and I shall have done wrong if I make it appear so. We were wild creatures of the woods too, as wild as the young dormice, who have their home in bramble bushes, where they retire, as they think in their foolish, self-centred, half grown-up way, from the world. They do not retire from the world, because, of course, their home is part of the world. So our home was our natural home, and our games were our natural games, and we were children of nature, as subdued to nature as the fishes are to water. But human thought and memory, whether they are deceptions or not, seem to detach a man from his world, and to make even that nature of which he is a part appear objective and a second thing. So now I see the world, and that joyous creature is myself, and yet no longer part of me.

You do me wrong if you suppose that this is mere talk: that birds were really no more to us than mindless inhabitants of a world where we were proud to be aliens. There *was* a brotherhood, and I will tell you how I first found out about it.

After ten years of waking every morning to hear starlings uttering sarcastic shrieks and whistles from the gutters and chimneys; after ten years of that almost continuous sparrow chip-chipping that goes on in the trees and outhouses and about the roofs of old country houses; after ten springs of thrushes' assertive artistry, and blackbirds' musing experimental, then practised, and finally triumphant, tone sketches, done entirely for the blackbirds' own pleasure; after a hard winter when we trapped and killed and roasted one of these very blackbirds; there came a certain summer day, well to be remembered now. We had begun to tire of bows and arrows at last, and four of us—John and I and two South African boys named Clifford and Spencer (who were at that time as good as extra brothers)—found, on a summer holiday afternoon, idleness upon our minds. What to do was the great question, and nobody had an opinion about it, till Clifford with a wild abandon, sick of idleness, suddenly cried out: "Let's go out and throw stones at birds!" So we agreed, without an ounce more cruelty than boys have by nature.

I don't think anyone of us took this to be the title of a purposeful occupation; it only meant not hanging about discussing occupations in that stale little workshop. We swung out. Stones were there to hand in the rough path that passed the door; and Clifford, who saw, at one time, a sensible stone to pick up, and a tiny wren in a plum tree thirty yards away, snatched up the stone, swung his arm and killed the wren. It was as though a normal and unsuspecting boy suddenly found himself able to perform miracles. We gasped with amazed laughter, and ran to the wren. Its little entrails lay shining in the hot sun. Its eyes were shut, its beak was caught in the act of crying, death took it in the middle of a breath; and certainly it was dead—still—small—harmless—and brotherly, we suddenly saw. There was a pain at the back of my mind, as though something shameful had been done, and the day not shamed by it. However foolishly, we all felt at that moment that we were cruel, careless fools. We had been idle, and the wren was dead. I was surprised that this should make me so sad, and in a boy's dim way I knew (rather to my confusion) either that I was soft-hearted about the creatures, or that they were dreadfully equal with us. A few more stones were thrown, but no more death was dealt, and all the afternoon I could not quite shake off a repressed horror. It was suddenly revealed to me what terrible power we had. In a vague, illogical way I saw then, for the first time, that it was a pity, from a bird's point of view, that his life should suddenly end. The contrast between life and death had become real and tragic, though only by means of the death of a wren. I remember, some years before, I had been chasing a cock, and in the fury of the chase had thrown a piece of wood wildly at him. It had struck him on the side of the head. He whirled foolishly round and round for a few seconds and then dropped—dead, as I thought. The guilt that I had felt after that stroke was not of murder, but of disobedience. I left him there, but I feared only for myself, lest my father should find out that by my act he was one chicken short. I didn't tell a soul; and it can be imagined what release from guilt I felt, when, the day afterwards, I saw the same fellow clucking to the hens over the dead ashes of a bonfire, and none the worse for my blow.

This was not murder; and I was, at that point of life, too young to have much imaginative sympathy. The apparent death of the cock had merely threatened to expose me. Now, at the death of the wren, I was three or four years older, and a new and troublesome faculty had been awakening. Through all those long days of our first decade beauty had shone about us and love had poured itself into us, largely unknown to us because we had never known the absence of these things. The spirit had silently been preparing that we might bear sorrows, and that very moment, when we looked at the dead wren (though there were others no doubt, less memorable), becomes the moment of initiation. I began to hate the waste of flowers picked and thrown away, and to feel myself guilty for slashing at nettles, or parsley heads or bluebells with a stick. There was one occasion when, with a small rifle, which John had borrowed, I fired at a bumble bee who was going the rounds of blackberry blossom by the wood; and all the pleasure of pride in a truly marvellous aim was lost in the wave of regret that assailed me for smashing with a bullet a life like the life of the summer itself. I began to hate myself for catching and killing summer butterflies, and for taking birds' eggs. We used to believe, with other country children, that to kill a beetle would bring rain; and in our innocent days we blamed one another for killing beetles—not because of waste or cruelty, but because we liked fine weather. Now when I was just able to understand the absurdity of the notion, I was almost willing to believe in its justice. I hated the sudden interference of conscience in many ordinary games and occupations. Such sensibility is a sickness of growing-up, too often the expense of spirit in a waste, and, sometimes I think, the beginning of our long estrangement from natural life. Pity is too easily indulged, life too easily turned in upon itself. After the dawn of this new light of consciousness our steps are necessarily further and further away from the barbarous but natural life of children, where impulse is immediately transformed into action, and the child is a simple manifestation of life in proper action, not capable of wickedness or virtue, neither body nor soul, but a life unable to divide itself (as we do to our unhappiness) into the considered and the considering. But I must dismiss this difficult subject.

You unfortunate people who live in towns laugh and lose patience with country folk because they seem to triumph every year (in the newspapers) about the cuckoo. Yet you hate winter, and ought to feel relief when we send our news to you. We did not hate winter, or any season; but we loved the turn of the seasons. Whenever the late hawkbits began to come out, and nuts to ripen, and leaves to dry up brown, whenever a mist began to form in Combourne valley at nightfall; or, at the beginning of the year, whenever some one luckier than the rest found the first primrose, or a piece of blackthorn or a solitary periwinkle, change was coming we knew,

and an adventure in it. While you were still but-
toning your overcoats against the rigours of winter,
we were finding these prophetic trifles, and even
in the end of January we were listening for a new
note in the thrushes' voice. So the spring's coming
was delightful just as a surprise is delightful, but
yet it was no surprise. Its slowness made us patient,
but, as one can only find a first flower once, the
discovery of spring came in a series of gentle
surprises, and we played a game of pretence within
ourselves, saying: "Look, look a primrose at last!"
though by all laws we knew the first primrose was
already due. In the early part of every year we were
able to find wonder enough in such commonplaces,
till the day's sun grew warm, and the banks (that
had been steadily covering themselves these last
four weeks) grew suddenly green and flourishing,
and milkmaids and arums and periwinkles were not
trophies any longer, and celandines, indeed, were
beginning to pass off. Late in our spring the Cuckoo
came—and called us to remember the warm days
and outdoor activities of summer soon to follow.

The world is full of struggling life and joy, sup-
pressed and not flaunted, to be inferred and felt,
not as yet to be seen. The world is full of power, and
yet all hushed, hesitating on the edge of beauty
visible, full of promise, waiting, whispering, ex-

pectant, awed by its own sensations, pregnant, wondering what stirs. Something is happening; but what is happening? They say that beauty is stirring and secret life ascending, but what are these? We were part of earth and nature, so that the world's excitement was in us. We, too, would wake early; we would not go to bed; we waited for something, only we did not know what it might be.

Then early one morning, with the sun across the trees, we heard a double call, and in an instant, recognizing, we ran to hang out of the window. In the woods between Combourne and Hor-Den we had, with all the insurgent earth, found our spirit's voice. It was the cuckoo, who resolved everything. The Mallions Woods answered him faintly half a mile away, Pine Woods and Mabs Wood heard, then Little Combourne and Ladys Den and the woods on Winchet Hill.

In a day or two the whole under-sky was hollow, ringing with its call and echo and answer; there was nothing in the earth and the still, even face of the sky, but this mysterious voice. This is sober matter-of-fact. Before I was eight I found I could not bear to hear it and remain alone. How little we were, and how lost, when the big world broke into voice and called that soft, monotonous, hazy call, here and a mile away, and nothing answered it but empty silence and its own echoes. It is terrible to be in an ecstasy of joy alone. All the hordes of life were united in a single cry, earth was no longer a mass of separate lives, but one spirit, crying out to be heard; and all its answer was its own voice repeated from some sunken valley on the other side of the hill.

I was in the children's gardens, alone on the top of our hill, when first the cuckoo's voice assured me of that secret spirit in our woods. I had surmised it before, but now that it was vocal I listened with a growing fear. At last I could not bear it. Dropping my spade, I tore down the path past the summer-house and greenhouse to be near the cheerful mortal sounds of kitchen and scullery. Yet when I arrived there I only wondered at my own fears, and though I could not go back to the garden, I would not go indoors.

What do explanations really explain? You may say that this is some phobia, some dread of being alone; you may say (what is, indeed, obvious) that this so-called spiritual voice of earth is only the call of a bird; that the feeling of power held in check, imputed to the senseless earth, is only a false translation of the child's own feelings. Physical knowledge can separate the parts of a spring morning in this world of mine, belittling in a sense, by descending from the one great to the many small, reducing the day to a million details—but what is a great fear in a little boy's heart? Or why should I feel a change in the world when the cuckoo sang unseen? Did I invent the god to account for the fear? The god may be poorly invented, but the fear was real. I did not invent that; it was caused by something. I knew that I was not afraid of the cuckoo, but afraid of what its cry meant. I knew what it was; I only vaguely felt what it meant, and now which of these was reality?

If you have watched a storm at night, though with a sharp scientific eye, counting its seconds, calculating its approach, and assuring yourself that it is an electrical disturbance due to the disorganization of electrons during the simple process of evaporation, have you not felt, when the great crash came, the exhilaration of fear, as though shaken by some power which would not be detailed into nothing, the very living Reason Why the separation of electrons should so manifest itself? If you cut a slice of bread into four, you do not quarter the Bread of it. No knowledge can whittle away the majesty of a storm, and we are little better than Greeks when we ask what majesty is. So all knowledge plays on the shores of the unknown, but a god shows himself to the soul of man, the soul which was born with the wit to know him, and was never sent to school, but went to school in a dream.

History of early childhood is really a list of first occasions, a list of minute discoveries whose significance was felt but not understood then, a list of new experiences. For the germ of spiritual life with which we began can only grow as it gets nourishment from the world in which it was sparked, and of its food it makes its own bulk. Its food is experience. I know that I was more myself after that shock of experience when first Our Wood was cut down; more myself after I had felt awe of the cuckoo. But smaller events than these have nourished me too. I remember how, one day, in the chapel meadow, in the long mowing-grass, I found a big blue flower, of a purity of colour comparable without loss with the blue of the sky. It was a big, rayed flower, like a blue sun, and it grew on a stiff, angular and almost leafless stalk. I looked at it till I could not bear it, for I was alone; and then I broke it off, stem and all, and hurried away to find Miss Bee, our mistress then; for the flower was a miracle to me, something rich and strange, and I had to register my discovery (I suppose) on a mind not my own, to be sure that it was credible. But before I found her my flower had faded quite out of its beauty by the heat of the summer afternoon, and it refused to revive in the water I gave it; so that I have always felt a little as though I was robbed of half my experience. But what is clear now, is that this joyful simple discovery left me changed. I am, even to-day, thirty years away from that blue succory bloom, partly what I am because I found it then, with my eyes for my spirit. And every cloud that I saw go marching mysteriously by across the heavens, and every silent summer instant in the fields that has impressed me, every first primrose or white violet that surprised me, every incident in fact that I remember now, had some addition to make. Often I cannot trace the addition, more often still I fail to give it a name, but I am sure that the very fact that I remember it proves that it nourished life in me, and is part of me and indestructible.

What is the good of such a life? Though I have all these memories, how do they serve the world of men, I asked myself? If I could only set them down for others, then the world might let me live a little longer. They are not much, but they are something which the world may have by my labour, and could not have without me. If I was luckier in my earth than many thousands, I am to try to leave them the shadowy forms of my joys, to wrestle with the angel of childhood till he tells me his secret, and then I am to put that down, truthfully, for a particular addition to the joy of the world. If there could be an invocation in prose I ought to invoke the cuckoo now, who was so high in the heaven of joy as to have the tips of his wings in terror, that others might borrow a baby's soul for a page or two, and tremble and begin to run away. Or I would call down the snow for you, not merely cold and yellow and imprisoning, not that at all, but the eager white desirable, so beautiful alone as to be immaculate, miracle-working, silent, royal and impartial. Or I would change fingers with you, and let you steal raspberries and gooseberries, and white currants on a string like an unfastened necklace, so that you would remember, this grown-up year, not only the taste of them, not only the theft, but their light leaves and rough leaves and thorns, and your hand going in among them, going in through a checker of sun and leaf-shadow, to steal them from their bushes.

13

Near Neighbours

THE people who lived round about us were all part of the spectacle of life: their existence admitted of no question or criticism; we were born to them, and during the long eternity of childhood they seemed to remain unchanged. There was a simple rightness about existence then; we accepted the world, and had not yet reached that unhappy age of comparison between things real and things ideal, which does so much to discredit the world. It was as though we had only one window from which to regard the whole process of life, and neither our godlike grandfather, nor Jimmy the Timber Merchant, nor Mr Baden the Universal Provider, ever appeared to us as creatures in any way alterable, or like ourselves. We did not perceive that they had their moods or their private life, and we certainly never thought of them as having grown up into their present (perfectly satisfactory) position from imps such as we were. With established regularity, as the sun moved in heaven, Jack Bateman dug in the garden and brought the sprouts to the kitchen; his big bent knife had only one blade, but that was so sharp that it could cut through a garden stick in one clean cut. He was the general odd-job man at school before Harry Excell's time, and if you got down at your very earliest in the winter, there you would find Jack sweeping the great schoolroom by candlelight, with all the desks pushed back into a crowded disorder; and when you went to bed at night you would pass by Jack in the washhouse, pumping rain water by the big pump, bowing and rising before the candle, and he would stop as you went by, to answer your good-night. There was a twinkle in his eyes then that was half candlelight and half a wicked and attractive humour. I can see him plainly now: a big man, a hot man—his face shone with it and his neighbourhood was moist and warm—and a very reliable friend. We bothered him with all our requests; we wanted string or sticks or a nail, we wanted a ball retrieved from the roof gutter, we wanted our garden dug or anything broken mended, and we went with complete confidence to Jack. He was even-tempered; he wore the perfect yokel's curl oiled down on his forehead, he nearly always lived in shirtsleeves, his eyes were never quite serious; any request of ours gently amused him, and giant as he was he could comfort a child with a bumped head as well as any woman we knew, except our mother. Somehow it never occurred to us that we were in the way when we were with him, and so we liked to be with him. I have spent many a happy summer afternoon in the hot shed where he cleaned boots and knives. But the best amusement came on Saturdays, when, after receiving our half-penny pocket-money at dinner-time, we would sit on the bank or the steps or the low brick wall, clutching the sweets we'd bought, and watch Jack Bateman "do the bricks." The yard from the front gate to the back door at school was paved with bricks laid in sand, and once every week, with a stiff broom and buckets of bright water, Jack would scrub them down. The glorious floods of water, the grand extravagance and carelessness of his way of throwing it, the crisp swish of the broom that drove the flood before it and left the bricks all glittering and red and clean—these things fascinated us. Whenever we were with him, too, we chattered all the time. He was part of our life, a big and pleasant part; but how strange it is, even now, to recognize that we were only part of his. He had his wife and son and daughters, his own fireside, his own garden, his evenings at the Woolpack, his Sunday mornings (let it be whispered) in the woods, and in all this we had no part at all. For all that we thought, he ceased to be Jack Bateman so soon as he passed out of the range of our little window, and it was always with a shock of surprise that we met him, as we rarely did, on Sundays in the road. He had his coat on, his Sunday best, and his best cap, and a flower in its peak or over his ear, and his face was pink with soap and shaving. We were shy in such a presence, and did not quite know how we stood with him.

His wife was a small thin woman, but his daughters were the loveliest of our village girls, inheritors, I think, of that quality in their father's nature which made his eyes twinkle. Their mother's voice was shrill and often raised to rebuke them. We, who only knew Mrs Bateman by her thin and staring face and sharp-edged voice and her startling way of wishing us good-morning, put her down as a minor terror, and never took kindly to her.

The Batemans lived in one half of a pair of ivy-covered cottages, next to Mr Baden's shop. Their neighbours were the Brumlys, an older couple, whose two sons, grown-up, were doing well for themselves in Canada. Mrs Brumly, in contrast to Mrs Bateman, had the Mrs Noah figure, that is she was narrowish in the waist but plump above and below. Her face was brown and smooth, her eyes were bright, and her mouth was sunken. Smiling was her first advance, and her only defence. She smiled so constantly that I found it impossible to imagine what she looked like in serious moments, when she was alone, or when, say, she had turned away from us on her own reddled doorstep, and had shut herself in by the parlour door. All the women helped in the fields at haymaking time; they worked in a long line across the field, walking backwards, and tedded the hay with their long new wooden rakes. Mrs Brumly's short, pronounced shape was easily recognized there, though all their faces were lost in the shadows of their big limp harvesting hats. Mrs Brumly's conversation was equally compounded of words and what would have been described as giggles had she been young or a woman you disliked. She twittered and chirped like a bird. Her husband was a mild, serious man whose face was almost completely covered in by a soft brown beard and whiskers; he was the country antithesis to Bateman, who gave an impression of strength and confidence. Mr Brumly's gentleness seemed to express a physical inferiority; his frame was small, his voice was far back in his beard, and he never volunteered even a passing good-day: only if you spoke, he spoke. They had lived a frugal, quiet life together; they never quarrelled and Mrs Brumly did not gossip. He went out daily to his farm work, cold or hot, wet or dry, at six o'clock in the morning, and might be met returning along the lanes any evening at half-past five. His pace, going or coming, was the same. He never looked hot or tired or glum, and he always spent his evenings at home. You couldn't even suspect him of poaching, he was so mild. No neighbour suspected them of hoarding, or, indeed, thought of money at all when they were by; but it must have occurred to some unprincipled rogue that so quiet a life meant thrift, and so stay-at-home a life suspicion of the world's way of taking care of riches. Anyhow, in the hop-picking season, when they were both necessarily away at work in the gardens, thieves broke into their cottage and robbed them. Then, in their dismay, they let the neighbours know that the whole of their savings of forty years—getting on for a hundred pounds—had been all that time hidden in a box in their bed. The thieves had discovered this and stolen it. A hue and cry was raised, and after some weeks a youth was arrested at Maidstone, but all that remained of their small fortune was a pound or two in his pocket, and a grey knave of a donkey that he had bought from gipsies. Mr Brumly had no trust in banks, and nobody, no cottager in our honest country, ever dreams of insurance; and so he lost all. On any of the days following this robbery Mr Brumly rose at six and returned at half-past five, grunted his usual reply to your good-days, and patiently plodded on;

not a sign of grievance or worry about his loss showed in his eyes—the rest of his face could not be expected to alter, for it was completely covered by that soft brown beard.

But Mrs Brumly in her soft voice repeated the tale in its brief details, when gossips drew her into it, a dozen times a day for a month. When I heard I was sorry that Mrs Brumly should be robbed, but I could not help a thrill of excitement about the donkey. What would they do to the thief, I thought, and what would become of the grey donkey? Would it be sent down here to Mr Brumly, for it was plainly his? But the donkey never came.

Beyond the Green, and Mr Baden's shop, was Jimmy's timber-yard, full of the trunks of trees, a natural playground, and a source of wonder, when, once every year, the itinerant steam sawmill (consisting of Edith, an unwieldly steam-traction engine, a long saw-bench and a hut on wheels where the sawyers lived) came down to cut up the year's harvest of trees into planks and gate posts. Jimmy was a good and skilful timber-merchant, who could look at a living tree and tell its weight, its quality and its value by a kind of instinct. He was an old man— never anything else to us—with the beard of a prophet in the family bible, and a ponderous and careful manner of walking. He was very deaf, and seemed to think that all the world was deaf too, for if he met any acquaintance abroad, the whole road would ring with exchange of greetings—the morning has often heard his thundered opinion of its weather. To children and women, however, he gave no words, but a small sideways jerk of the head. He was a grey shaggy man, very broad and big; his eyebrows were like other men's moustaches. He looked like a giant, but everyone knew that (like Achilles) he suffered with tender feet, and he kept a truss of dry hay at home, from which he would pull a wisp every morning to wear in his boots. It seems a strange palliative; it certainly could not be called a remedy, for the tenderness of his feet remained with him, and created a way of walking that seemed to be part of his character. His steps were very wide and slow; his dialect was rich, difficult and heavy, and his features were hidden under shagginess—all these seemed to be the bodily signs of a slow and weighty soul.

Jimmy's house was at the Green itself, separated from the Brumly's by Strange's cottage, and about three hundred yards down the road from the timber-yard. It was bigger and slightly more pretentious than the surrounding cottages, an old house too, but fitted with a new and more urban painted wooden front. In the garden before the house grew standard roses, pinks, sweet-williams, wallflowers, lilies, and a castor-oil plant (which children eyed with a sickly and familiar curiosity). A low fence of white paling divided this garden from the road, and on the lower side of it, a high plank fence leaned over the bank, and an apple tree and a plum tree leaned over the fence. At the bottom of this fence a double plank gate led into the wood-working shed where the farmers' gates were made.

In this house and garden Jimmy lived with his wife for fifty years, and then she died. It was their sorrow that they had no children. While his wife lived he was a regular "worshipper" and a familiar figure in my grandfather's chapel. Every Sunday his wooden pew loudly cracked as he sat down to pray; but after he was left a widower he was never seen there again. Those who knew this old man intimately may, perhaps, guess at the meaning of that change. Whether it was an unwillingness to arouse the old tenderness (for they always came to chapel together) or a defiant denial of God's goodness, or a relapse of despair, or a new freedom, I do not know. After a time a widow, a London relation, came down to the country to keep house for him; for his domestic affairs had been allowed to fall into a bad state by his indifference, though the timber-yard did not suffer. She was very deaf too, liable to weep at the mention of the least pleasure or sorrow, would remark, with tears in her eyes, what a lovely morning it is. And she still bravely struggles with the self-neglect of the old man. Her exact relationship to Jimmy has never been defined: she calls him Oncle and he calls her Antie!

The wooden cottage above Jimmy's house, and next to Mrs Brumly's, was divided into two. In a flash of memory it comes back to me that I have been inside one of these houses, and I remember that the room was small and very warm, and that it seemed full of furniture, some of which was painted white. I can see the bright fire again, and smell the smell of the lamp upon the table; I can hear the whining voice of Mrs Strange asking me in, and I can see Strange himself, most surprising glimpse of all, looking up over steel spectacles from his paper, smiling at me under his uncultivated moustache. He was sitting near the fire, in shirtsleeves for comfort, and it was the first time I had ever seen him without his cap. We came singing carols, and were to be given an apple each. As it was my turn to knock, I had come all alone up the short brick path to their door, while the others waited, giggling in the dark; but the only memory that remains to me (one of those pictures without a story, like all very early memories) is the room, as I have described it. Who those others were, or what other adventures we had that Christmas Eve, I cannot recall.

Strange was the carpenter of the place. He was a figure perfectly familiar to me in his working clothes covered with chips and sawdust. He came to school to do our many repairs; but if it was a broken window in the drawing-room to be mended, or a bed in one of our more private bedrooms, wherever he went, his cap went with him too. He was the man (there is one in every village) who was distinguished by a high voice like a woman's voice. But if his voice was pitched high, his wife's was higher still. Moreover, she loved singing, and helped at all tea-meetings, mothers-meetings, children's meetings and anniversaries at grandfather's chapel, where her thin and glassy treble could be heard high above the united voice of all the congregation, beating against the boarded ceiling, and, in a manner of speaking, turning dizzy somersaults about the iron tie-bars of the roof. She was a small woman, plumper than Mrs Brumly, but of the same shape. She is most familiar to me in her place at the long trestle tables, when the Sunday schoolroom smelt sweetly of shop-cake, jugs of hot tea and pyramids of bread-and-butter. She was, as they say, one of the "workers" at the chapel, but not in the spiritual sense. Nobody was quicker at cutting long loaves into thick slices, nobody better at making tea in a copper, and on the day of any great meeting, when all the countryside came to tea at fourpence a head, Mrs Strange was early there, in her black hat and white apron, running about from outhouse to vestry, now lighting the copper fire, now setting out the blue and white cups in mass formation at the pouring-out end of each long narrow row of tables. Then, while all the congregation sat out the drowsy afternoon sermon, Mrs Strange hummed in the vestry as though there was nothing sacred about its pitch-pine and pointed windows, almost giving the place a secular tea-shop air, except that she never took off her hat. Long baker's loaves waited beside her in baskets. She stood at her work, clasping a loaf to her bodice, spreading the butter like an artist, and cutting each slice through to her very apron with a sharp, flexible knife. She was the quickest fingered of women—her fingers seemed to be possessed with lives and a will and skill of their own.

She was good at a tea-party or a sewing-meeting, but she was best of all in the hop garden, where her mittened fingers flew in and out among the rough hop leaves, over and under and in between, snicking off hops clean of all leaves as though they had instinct for nothing but hops, while she, above them, carried on a rapid conversation from under her hat with Mrs Larkin, two bins away, her hands like the hands of another picker, working away surely (though blindly) below the cross-pole.

Mrs Strange loved gossip, and worked best where she talked most; in good hops she picked forty bushels a day where the quieter women could pick no more than thirty.

If you met her in the road you noticed that she took such small steps that her walk was almost a run, for she was always in a hurry, from one point of gossip to the next, and she would thrust out her sharp little chin and give you her good-morning in a shrill singing voice that had kindness, if not a curtsy, in its tune.

I am like one who has raised a troublesome ghost. It had been my intention to call in order on all the inhabitants, but I cannot dismiss the world that Mrs Strange brings with her. She in her way stands for all that world over which grandfather ruled as pastor and not as schoolmaster. It was, indeed, the whole of our social world, and the picture of Mrs Strange, cutting up for tea, has made my memory restive. I want to taste that tea again, and the sweet shop-cake, and the joys of anniversaries and summer treats.

There were five festivals in our nursery year: Christmas, your own birthday, the X, Bran-tub Day, and that winter anniversary of our Sunday School which we called simply Pieces. Bran-tub Day was the summer Treat, and we talked about it in the nursery for weeks before it came. Even when the day came there was the long morning to get through somehow, and it was difficult enough, though necessary, to pretend that it was a normal morning of lessons and play. The thought kept knocking at your mind and would not let the day be common. But then when dinner-time came, and we had to store away our slates and leave the school-room empty, every act that pointed to the undoubted end of all lessons at twelve o'clock was done to the tune of exultant anticipation. As we left our little school-room we felt its bareness like a joy. Every vestige of school had been hidden. In an hour or so Mrs Strange would be getting the tea ready in that very room; as we ran home, too, we had to skirt the hedges of the cricket field, and though it was empty at noon, by half-past two it would be full of little boys in new and odorous corduroys, and little girls in white starchy pinafores, and we should be there, and it would be Bran-tub Day in truth.

How bright the sun was and how hot the afternoon, when we, in our best clothes, went out and climbed the five brick steps to the gate and heard it shut behind us with that sharp, wooden latchless clack it had. Our Sunday clothes assured us of the day's importance—our sailor blouses had stiffened collars that reached out to the shoulders and hung down squarely at the back, under our chins the Sunday elastic pulled upwards, so that our Sunday clothes and the sight of that holiday crowd below us, together made a paradox and lifted the day to the mood of a miracle. For clothes, to the boys of us (at least to me), were important, not for the figure we cut in them, but for the mood we put on with them. There was something enjoyably wrong when we wore our ordinary clothes on Sundays, and something formal but unique when we wore our Sunday clothes to games and other secular joys.

Our shyness made us stand together for a while under the great trees at the top of the field. The ground fell away gently to a wide green plain, and there about sixty or seventy children were already assembled, making a great noise. In the corner nearest to the pond Miss Bee had collected most of the girls, and they had joined hands in a big ring, and were chanting one of the singing games of our part of the country.

> Willy Willy Wall-flower growing up so high,
> We're all maidens and we shall all die:
> Excepting Betty Martin, she's the only one;
> She can hop and she can skip
> And she can turn the candlestick.
> Turn her round the other way....

At this point Betty Martin unclasps her hands and turns in her place in the moving ring of dancers—but the song never stops—while she is turning, the dancers begin again in a wailful tune with Willy Willy Wallflower, and so on and on, in a monotony of which only the grown-ups weary, till everyone is facing outwards and red in the cheeks with singing and dancing. The little boys played with the girls, but the bigger boys, already half-way to yokels, could never be properly organized; while some played cricket others devoted most of the afternoon to a round of teasing and shouting and were continually being cautioned by the severe but helpless Sunday School teachers.

In and out of this noisy crew my black-coated grandfather moved. He (it was unthinkable!) never joined in the games himself, but with his very smile he seemed to bring us fine weather, and he looked out the shy ones, or the crying ones, or the lonely ones, and honoured them with a peppermint just as if they had been his own grandchildren. At five o'clock he would go to the lower stile and clap his hands loudly to call us in for tea; and this, of course, is where Mrs Strange came in. She was there (with my mother and an aunt or two as well) sending girls to their places at the long tables. Boys went in at the back door and sat scornfully apart, for in a body like that they felt strong and superior and thought it their duty to despise girls. But they were quiet as soon as tea began. Here, as at the Farm, grandfather would make us sit and sing our grace before beginning. The chatter went on and on, everybody's appetite in those days was hearty; Mrs Strange renewed the plates of bread-and-butter and cake, while other responsible people poured out sweet tea for each child. At last it was time to go again, but before we went we had another grace to sing, and grandfather made us a little grandfatherly speech. What else he said no one could remember now, but when, at the end of it, he made some mention of the Bran-tub, a spell of anticipation fell on the company, which broke in riot a few minutes later. Boys snatched their caps from the forms and tore shouting through the chapel yard, back into the meadow. Then the races were run and the prizes were awarded, and at last, when the babies of the party had almost given up hope, they were so tired, my father and my uncle were seen at the wicket gate on the far side. All eyes watched their long slow progress over the grass, for they carried between them a big zinc bath—the Bran-tub—from which the whole day took its name.

So all we children lined up in two lines of boys and girls, and as we slowly filed by the Bran-tub, we bared our right arms above the elbows, and each in turn plunged his arm deep into the warm dry bran. Hidden in the bran were parcels, and in each parcel was a toy—a doll, a trumpet, a wooden ship, a penny flute, a mouth-organ, a book of transfers, a box of coloured chalks. But while we drew up in line the sun was nearing the west, and there was barely time afterwards for a full comparison among us all of the presents we had received. Anxious mothers and elder sisters at the roadside were already claiming the youngest of the children. Grandfather was talking happily to groups of them, now in one place, now in another. Now games of all sorts were done with, and corners of the field sounded with the rivalry of new trumpets and whistles, while the boys and girls made for the particular stile which was the nearest way home for them, and climbed over into the road, and were nothing but receding voices and laughter, till even the sound of them all had gone. We had gone too, happily satisfied and tired, still talking of our presents as though there were nothing else in all the world. But Bran-tub Day was over now, and the future, with school to-morrow, looked flat and dull before us. It would come round again, of course, in a year—but then how long a year appeared.

When the voices of children are heard on the green,
And laughing is heard on the hill,
My heart is at rest within my breast,
And everything else is still.
"Then come home, my children, the sun is gone down,
And the dews of night arise;
Come, come, leave off play, and let us away
Till the morning appears in the skies."

14

Christmas Day

AUTUMN, I suppose, had taken us by usual surprise; we had been busy chattering with the Summer, and had not dreamt that she was leave-taking, when unexpectedly she dropped our hand, and turned, and here was her freckled follower, that changeful season.

On a day in any autumn someone—(probably Stella)—was sure to exclaim, "Only six weeks, and then it will be Christmas!" And the year itself suffered a shock at such words, sheared into unequal parts: a vast, crowded past; but how tense and brief a future.

Christmas was the natural climax of any year. For John and me, for Stella and Carrie and those of the small fry who had any power at all over time, there were two such days and no more in every year— birthday, and Christmas Day. These had the closest association in our minds, though the only factor common to both was this receiving of presents. Nobody under fourteen had any doubt about the matter. It was not greed. We depended for our possessions entirely upon gifts, and chiefly upon what fell to our lot on these two generous days.

The penny that came on Saturday was improvidently spent on Saturday; and even so simple a necessity as a pocket-knife was beyond hope of purchase. Thus, also, with pencils and rubbers, rich crayons and paints, drums, whips, hoops, printing outfits, pistols, autograph albums, telescopes, compasses, snakes-and-ladders, balls, carpentry sets (to speak only in a masculine way) and suchlike necessities. We were bound to be dependent upon presents; an unfortunate Christmas meant an ill-equipped life; it meant borrowed paints, hunting for someone to sharpen a pencil, handicaps.

Christmas being so all-important, Stella's discovery (if it was Stella's) at once gave Time a strange double reality: the ominously brief days still dawned and dawdled, died and succeeded one another, and Christmas drew nearer and yet no nearer, and yet again drew nearer. We were, for instance, continually forgetting it—in the prolific and useless harvest of elm leaves along the road and in the playground, in bonfires on Saturdays, in the startling strangeness which solid white morning fogs bestowed on a well-known world, in frost on spider-webs, in the first aching nip of winter that brought fires into school —and then, suddenly, examinations, leading through a day's disorder, to Last Day at school. We lived at school; the others went home. One stood, that morning, in an echoing, fireless schoolroom, all lessons over; but one almost heard Christmas galloping down at last, no more than six or seven days ahead.

And the six or seven seemed so short precisely because there was so much to be done; for it need not be said, that, as distinct from birthdays, Christmas was, in the matter of gifts, everybody's birthday. Aunts one merely noticed in May both generously gave and rightly received presents at Christmas time; and no one wished to shirk responsibilities. Christmas was always a joint effort, and a joint enthusiasm. Even at six a child could, and would, fold pointed paper "hair-tidies" or spills, or blanket-stitch a kettleholder. At the least everyone could, and many did, paint easy plum puddings and holly for cards for the last remembered. There was fever of work and secrecy in those last days, until the afternoon before Christmas, when blessed with permissive weather, we got together the pence we had come by, and an extra sixpence or so from relenting parents, and we set out to walk the two miles through the winter lanes over the hills to shop at Gowdhurst.

I cannot go into the arithmetic, which was simply the problem of suiting as many relatives as remained unsuited (a variable) out of a small and definite, and hampering total. But rare country shops had an atmosphere above arithmetic in those days—an intimacy and a clustering bounty, cheerful and anything but reticent—which depended largely upon the acceptable combined ignorances of architecture, electricity, salesmanship, or good taste. I am not sure whether Miss Button's shop was built for a shop or merely "thrown out" or just converted. To us it was unquestionable and right. It was a small triangular room, with the door (automatically ringing a shaker bell as you entered) at the pointed end.

If it had been purposely built for a shop, the architect had not thought to consider what kind of a shop, indeed Miss Button herself clearly felt no limits of that sort, except food—she never stocked food. Thus her place, helped by the hot air of a Gothick lamp-stove, had a dry and drapery smell. Ribbons, I should say—ribbons and lace—hairpins, hatpins, collar-supports—were characteristic of the all-the-year-round Miss Button; but all such gear as this was swept out of her mind by the Christmas excess. Do you know those limp, canvas-bodied dolls, with shiny china-ware heads and necks, no clothes, but pointed black glossy heavy cold clicking french boots on the leg-ends? Miss Button had boxes of them. She had packs of parlour games, Snap, Happy Families, Ludo, crisp Dominoes, rattling Halmas, and of course such things as marbles (in tape-tied bags), lead soldiers (not much in our line), pop-guns, and wooden symbols of engines and horses so hardened in convention by an ancient ritual of toymaking that they bore no more resemblance to real trains and horses than the pegged knees and hips and flat bellies of wooden dutch dolls bore to our own well-known anatomies. But the smell, and then the touch, of newness was everywhere, and though drums and musical boxes were, as Miss Button knew, for ever out of reach of our purses, we might linger over them, see how they worked, enjoy them in all but the having. When at last we set out on the long walk home, easily carrying our parcels, we knew that the last turnstile had been passed. No more presents could be bought, no more now could even be finished off. It was supper and bed as soon as we had labelled the last of our packets and told our mother all, over the cocoa. Bed of course by candlelight, eagerly sought tonight; for we were to hang up our stockings. Carol singers faltered in the dark below us while we undressed and said our prayers.

Santa Claus was a game with us; we knew and respected the rules quite as well as the grown ups. They smilingly admonished; we knowingly responded. And when we were in bed, John and I, newly determined this time to see the thing through to the exact truth, did all we knew to keep awake.

There was always, in spite of our democratic large-family rationalism, just a chance. Though we knew it was not Father Christmas; who it was we did not know. But we graduated into sleep. (How did they know when we were asleep?)

We woke in black morning, long before day. We stretched out a groping hand to the stocking, and felt that weighty and angular sausage and brought it rustling in itself to bed. There was always an apple, an orange, a twist of sweets—tom-tit jellies sanded with sugar, and crescents and stars and circles of chalky peppermints. There was always a penny; also, perhaps a rolled sheet of transfers, a magnifying glass, or a little raffia basket. For Santa Claus—it was well devised—brought only delicate tokens, little fore-tastes to begin the day well. In a cold that we would not feel and in a darkness that added to our fingers' mystification, we went through the wrapped contents of our stockings, and knew everything, and had eaten most by the time that dawn arrived.

It was characteristic of Christmas Day that, sharing a touch of both Sunday and weekday, it belonged to neither class. We put on clean linen and best suits without resentment; we found that we were not late for breakfast, because breakfast (for once) was smilingly waiting for *us*, in sustenance a normal breakfast, porridge and eggs, but eaten under the influence of the holly and ivy behind picture-frames, and towards the end transmuted by the loaded arrival of the postman with millions of cards and not a few pretentiously shaped parcels. Cards were distributed; parcels, by customary agreement, were put on the pile unopened.

Could it be true? We scattered from breakfast, and somehow filled in the long morning with Sunday School (where the collection gave us a penny instead of taking one from us), and a few suspiciously ordinary occupations. But when we got back— still too early for the fabulous Christmas dinner— someone had transformed the great school dining-room. A long wide board, covered with many white cloths, ran down the room. It was decorated with holly sprays, coloured papers, vases of chrysanthemums, towers of Blenheims and Cox's, boxes of candied figs with fragile leaf-metal servers, pyramids of mince pies, and enough cutlery and drink to serve nearly thirty people. For what is the use of living at a school in the holidays if you may not, on a Christmas Day, sit thirty down to dinner? It was of such a feast as this that I thought (and still think) whenever I read the parable of the marriage feast and the man without a wedding garment who was cast out—terrible thought—"and there shall be weeping and gnashing of teeth."

The bell sounded now, and from all quarters the people mustered immediately, threaded by children whose coiled-up excitement was beginning to have its way with them at last. We were seated, grace was sung, the menfolk were busy at the carving table, plates began to pass from hand to hand. Must I go on?

Singly, and at odd times during the significant fore-noon, Stella and John and I had, casually if we could, passed down that narrow, windowless passage out-side the Front Dining-room (this was its name; I never knew us dine there). The table had been taken away; more than twice its company of chairs now sat there unoccupied, vacant with expectation. The grate was prepared already with a hissing log fire. It was a dark, one-windowed room, low-browed but cosy. In a corner of its deepest twilight, piled up on the floor and half burying two great baskets, lay a quite un-countable heap of wrapped presents. In this room, at the classical right time, the middle movement of the great Christmas symphony would unfold; but before that moment, with all our will, but much against our heart, we had to accept the discipline of a walk. No doubt it began as a device to get the company away while the wreck of dinner was washed up and the table subtly altered for tea. But in my days the walk was official in its own right; Father came with us, a holiday-father, easy-humoured and primed with riddles. So we met the wind and saw the village empty by December daylight, for none of the cottagers had the ritual reason that we had to face the uncosy elements. There were no demurs; the day allowed for the discipline. By half-past three we crowded into the Front Dining-room, lit now by mixed firelight and soft lamplight.

The Mother (as Aunt Mary called her) was in her chair, her two or three babies (for safety against the strain of excitement) on footstools close to her; the rest of us anywhere. And, waiting his cue from the fall of silence among us, Father was in office by the pyramid and baskets.

His was the great part; he was the superb soloist, king in this movement, and he needed no help from red mantle or white whiskers. Father Christmas was a well-enough legend: Father himself was a reality. Through his lips every label on every parcel was given a voice. One at a time he picked them up and dwelt on them. He would be puzzled, or would make mistakes and correct them, or would talk tantalizingly and wrongheadedly about the largest packet—what it felt like or looked like, keeping the company in a tickle of tolerant excitement. He knew when to spin it out, and when to hurry it up, which packets must be handled with frightening care, and which neatly flung to the addressee's knees.

We loved it, as under his endless performance his hair grew disordered, his pretence more extravagant, and our spirits more varied and nearer riot. For now discipline properly began to give way. Strings were cut and papers publicly torn off, and still the fantastically unexpected parcels accumulated, and still were unwrapped, till the floor below became a sea, with billows of brown paper, and the cosy room, so Sundayish and dim on most days of the year, rang with exclamations of joy surprised.

At length, however, the pyramid had gone and the baskets were empty; Father's work was done. He had few parcels of his own, but he didn't seem to mind. Mother, of course, had her parcels; she had been the first on every list, even as far back as November, and she best liked the things we ourselves had made. I think it seemed redundant, if not presumptuous, to give presents to Father; and indeed the presents to Mother truly included him, and he accepted the intention even though Mother got the pincushion or the fretwork. And now, while we were yet caressing our treasures and demonstrating them, here he was collecting the string and the paper, tidying up.

By and by the girls began to whisper together, and then to go out; tea was in half-an-hour, and they had frocks to try—and, suddenly, the great third movement had ended, the room grew in half-way towards its own size again, the fire was mended, the lamp-wick was lowered, the afternoon's gains were piled and taken to quarters.

Daylight had gone long ago. Now, at last we and Christmas together were safely walled in by conspiring night. John and I, boys, and untroubled by the need for re-dressing, lightly enjoyed the brief hiatus alone, thought over again our presents one by one, waited watching the great logs oozing their spittle, said little, but found in each heart a great safety and content. We wandered out into the passage. Christmas was here indeed and at last; it was now, it was beginning.

Steal a glimpse, with us, at the long schoolroom. Though as yet the lamps are unlit, there will be fire-light enough from the two high fires in it. See all the chairs in order against the wainscot, see the soft feminine colours of paper chains looping down into the flamelight out of the high wooden ceiling. Notice the great boughs of holly and tots of berried ivy nailed above the mantels and above the doors and between the windows, dark and rich masses of luxuriant shape transforming the shadows. Look at the long trestle table laughing with dimpled oranges and apples, with dim bowls of nuts, and shut boxes of sweets.

Take this one look into the dancing dark and light,

and shut the door quickly, for there is a noise like tea-time; we hear girls' voices. Strangers, cousins and relations of the more distant sort, and Christmas partners from other houses, have come in out of the night—they say it is sprinkling with snow—and have hung up their wraps, and have kissed, and are moving down the steps to the big dining-room again.

The just perceptible grossness (shall I say) of the Christmas dinner-table is not a character of the tea-table. There is just as much to eat, but the food has art and charm and delicacy now, not merely alimentary goodness. Cakes are iced, biscuits are fancy, teacups and tea-urn have a twinkling, jewelled quality under coloured and shaded lamplight, and the crackers are there, things made with a charming excess, tufted, tinselled, lying (one over each plate) demurely yet. And there is chatter at tea. Surely, the afternoon's plunder has given everyone topics enough. Moreover, this time our visitors are guests, and deserve our smiling small-talk, and give as good as they get. There is no more hurry; this is time to spend: Christmas is here.

We move without haste from the tea-table at last, leaving the shaded lamps burning. Someone—some uncle—had preceded us, and the schoolroom, when we drift there, now seems blazing with extra lamps; the fires are twice themselves, well guarded against coming boisterousness within wire cages. With our Father as King again, and with Uncle Day and Uncle Ernest as his first ministers, we begin to sing games, we run games, we dance games, we shout games, we sit down to games, while the old folk, who have seen so many Christmasses, sit by and gossip absently, or, watching us, hold out a kind hand to catch the glow of the fires, and smile, thinking, approving.

In order of age and tiredness as the evening advances, one after one the children will be persuaded and withdrawn to bed. Soon it will be my fate, and John's, and we know it. We must now cheerfully climb the four steps out of the schoolroom and look back at the party that shows no dimming of light and mirth because of our leaving. The bedroom is cold; the heart is satisfied; and while we take to the sheets and understand that we really are tired, the noise and laughter comes faintly up the stairway still.

No Christmas is quite perfect, for each waits to be proved—and at the height of the tune they end.

What is there now to look forward to? Why is John creeping out of bed again? He calls me; he has looked out to the stars and the roof. "It's snowing," he whispers.

Snowing!

15

Early Morning

As a family, and a country family, we did not get up early. The labourer's breakfast was at six o'clock, but ours was never till eight o'clock. Even so we were often late to breakfast, and often reproved for it. Our pocket-money was then arranged under a new system to correct our late-to-breakfast habits—and my father decided that we should receive on Saturday a halfpenny for every morning early to breakfast. When this proved ineffective, we were sent to bed early too.

To be early to breakfast you had to be in your place when grace was said. An instant before grace was early, and an instant afterwards was late. Yet with all these devices we were great sinners, so that the idea of being up early in the morning was itself an idea of virtue, and, logically, the earlier you were, the greater the virtue. In the summer time, with breakfast at eight, there was thus left to us one adventure which, besides being enthralling and exciting in itself, also received (or so we argued) the pleasant blessings of our parents. So now and then, and especially at the beginning of the summer holidays, when the longest days always seemed to finish too soon, John and I would, on going to bed, sometimes decide that we were going to get up early. An old family servant was the earliest riser. Nothing would cure her of this habit. Summer and winter, as punctual as Greenwich, she would be down and start working by six o'clock. So, unless we meant to be extravagant in our earliness, we would go out of bed in our nightgowns, having made the decision, and call up the dark narrow stairs to the servants' bedrooms, to ask Liza to wake us both at six. What a difference between must get up and will get up! By quarter past six we were out in the cold air and hot sun, two of the happiest little devil-prigs in an empty world, rich in two golden hours stolen from to-day's purse when to-day was not expecting us. We probably went fishing, and came in wet to the ankles with dew, long after grace had been said at the breakfast table; but we did not lose our credit or our pocket-money, for the crime against which these laws worked was the crime of lying in bed, and we were in respect of such foolish sins two unbearable saints, expecting the company to listen to our achievements and adventures, only disguised from naked self-conceit by a decently modest manner.

Sometimes even six in the morning was not early

enough for our overnight ambitions, and then we had a special method of making sure that we would wake at the proper time. When we were ready to blow out the candle we would tell each other exactly how early we meant to be. Four o'clock or five o'clock? Say five o'clock for to-morrow. Then two entirely serious little boys would bang their heads hard five times against the wooden wall, blow out the candle, and go to sleep talking. Punctually at five, we knew, we should wake, and we did.

About the sunlight in the morning I used to notice a stillness and secrecy all its own. Our room, at the time I am remembering, had only one window, and the view from that was entirely of roofs. Highest of all was the new nursery chimney, which was bathed in the first upflow of light; below it were three separate roof-ridges, one on which the chimney stood, and two meeting it at right angles, with a valley gutter between them. The sky was clear and pale like pearl over these roofs. A starling sat on the nursery ridge, oily and freckled with silver in the sunlight, his feathers ruffled into points and ragged with bodily joy, and his whole being concentrated on quips and claps and hisses and long human whistles. The garden too, though not seen from the window while I was dressing, was very noisy with cheeps and chatterings of sparrows. It seemed so necessary to be quiet and quick that I scamped washing for fear of ringing the tin basin, and hastily pulling my jersey over my ears, and carrying my boots in my hand, I went out (John still asleep there) into a house where nobody else was awake. The stairs and passages, lit by an unappreciated daylight, all seemed to breathe and stir with a silence entirely different from the silence of a dark night, and far more active on its own account than the silence of an empty house. The rooms downstairs were cold, the blinds were down, the air was stale with last night, remains of supper littered the table, and the very arrangement of chairs and plates struck me as strange, for supper was a meal only known to me as a muddle of sounds; voices and the rattle of plates going on together for a long time by lamplight while we were in bed—almost a mystic ceremony at which, so far, I had never assisted. Now, in the young morning, every room was dim with its blinds or curtains drawn; extinguished lamps stood in their places on the tables. The fireplace in the kitchen was cold and empty except for a few grey ashes; the kettle was dead on the hob. Everywhere the place was oppressive, so that instinctively I walked on tip-toe, and felt the silence like an interdict against words. If I had spoken aloud, my voice, I know, would have frightened me. The kitchen clock ticked hard and loud, and in the emptiness the ticks even echoed a little. I drew the top bolt of the back door by standing on a chair. With a sense of delicious sin I stole a thick and already buttered slice of bread from the table, dipped it extravagantly, butter down, into a basin of sugar, and opening the door, hurried out into the solitude of day. The change from the confined and used-up air of the night into the dewy and sun-tingling air outside was as keen to my senses as a plunge into cold water. I took care to shut and latch the back door without a click, and then I climbed into the garden by the nearest way, and eating my sugared bread, stood for a moment overwhelmed by the riches which I had stolen from sleep. There was no whim but mine to consult, all laws of daylight were abrogated, and yet daylight was here and my own. The birds were certainly tamer and more numerous. Sparrows squabbled almost at my feet; for they were all accustomed to an early morning licence, as if the world were theirs before six by a law of Nature and time, without fear of disturbance. They did not quite believe in me, certainly they allowed me to come near to them—much nearer than in later hours. And everywhere there was the sense of a spirit or creature indifferent to human boys, a spirit who had slipped round out of sight by the snowberry hedge only a moment before, and when I followed, had, I felt, just escaped me again by going out to the road under the fir trees. I followed. Sheep grey with dew in a grey field browsed on without looking up at me; the starling on the nursery roof behind me shouted and hissed as though he did not see me; the sun was in a strange place, low and liquid, among the tops of the oaks by the Farm. The earth was wide awake and noisy and very much herself, but not a human sound or sign was perceptible. In the shadows the clean and dustless air was aching cold—the dew was colder than frost on my shoes—and, walking from the shadow of a hedge into the sunbeams, I could feel the warm rays like a substance touch my eastern cheek and my right hand. I was cold even in my own shadow, but I was King, alone, in an unsullied land.

As I walked along the gritty road and turned up under the cedar tree by the chapel, I again felt that mingling of joy and fear which is ecstasy. There was no wind, yet the ground under the oak trees was dark with drippings of dew from the golden young leaves. It was early summer. I passed a steep bank by the ale-house garden. It was deep with rank grass, nettles, goose grass, hedge-garlick and new vetches; in the angles between leaves and stems heavy dew lay in drops, but a path worn by the feet of village children led barely through these grasses to a natural doorway, and this led into a wood where I had never ventured. I climbed the bank and looked in. As yet the level sun had not shone in, and the place was a dark cavern with its roof supported by thousands of slender pillars, and in that darkness nothing could grow but wild parsley, fools' parsley, which comes from nothing to a flower in a week, so suddenly that its flat discs of white flowers are a yearly surprise. It grew deep and shadowy, away from this natural gate into the fastnesses of the wood, all its umbels standing at a level, a thin surface of parsley flowers whose stems were so numerous and so shaded that they stood to support them unseen, and the flower heads seemed to be floating in the still, dark air, a foot above the ground. But I was for sunlight and hilltops that morning and came down from the wood again to go on, up through the village.

This road by day was generally in the possession of neighbours, but now in Grove's cottage garden, although the washing still hung on the line, it hung there as if it had long been forgotten—the night had passed like a hundred years; it had swept the earth clean of her old possessors and left her free and incredibly young and gay. How could a boy feel this? Had I been asked when I returned, and

201

the others were there at the breakfast table, I should have stammered and said, "Oh, it was a lovely morning," I should not have added that it was so lovely that it made me afraid. What kind of joy it was can best be told, perhaps, by saying that I did not choose to repeat it often—never went out to assault the walls of the world of spirit, nor thought (as I have thought since) that if I wanted to experience that delight again, I had only to get up and out early on a summer morning. I have denied it by every law I know; I have said that what I breathed in as divine was but an unfamiliarity, that what I took to be exaltation was only my loneliness, that the world's excess of beauty was my own youth in my eyes; but though the moments are rare, and though the glimpse is a flash, times there are when a thousand common beauties strike and are one terrible annihilating sweetness together. I cannot express this early morning transfiguration of the earth except by saying that, at the instant of my advance a presence had just vanished from the place. This was why I went on tip-toe, and feared and exulted, though the words that I write now would have been like jargon to me then (and, indeed, they are now, yet I do the best I can). And this is not a later lyricism, for body claims more and the moments of sight grow less frequent with the gentle advance of years. The joy was stamped upon my childish mind, and—what may be significant—the fear as well; and the key picture of the morning that I am recalling is that dark, unvisited wood, grey with the lace-like level of its parsley flowers. I could not have gone in!

So I came down from the bank and idled my way past the ale-house, noting the busy air of the white cocks and hens in the garden under the great cherry tree, and past all the other houses still sleeping in the sunlight. A vole plumped loudly from the bank into the water of the cricket-field pond, and I stood to watch his arrow of ripples and his dark anxious nose as he advanced through the water towards the bank where I stood under the rusty hawthorn. Even he knew that the earth was safely self-possessed, and forgot his usual timidity, till I raised a hand to shade my eyes from the reflected light. Then with a single sound of water closing over him, he dived out of sight, and the ripples died away.

The houses that stood round the Green were all shut and silent too; they gazed, with their windows like eyes, as I went past. The only sound I heard here was the impatient thud of a horse's hoof upon the cobbles in Roberts's stable: one sharp heavy sound of iron on stone. I fancied the spark that he struck. The cobbler's shop was shuttered and asleep. Grass and parsley grew out of its thatching over the double door. It might have been asleep for a hundred years. In the meadow beyond Jimmy's timber-yard a shaggy pony stood knee deep in wet mowing grass and sorrel, fast asleep. The hedges were top-heavy with new luxuriant shoots: rose, honeysuckle, and black bryony vines clambered carelessly high and hung their delicate tips over, wet with dew, and waiting for a breeze, and the roadside grass strips were high with buttercups and big oxeye daisies. Now I was on the ten-foot road at the top of the hill, and had nothing but the sky over my head, cloudless like a great blue bubble, and the sun was free of the entanglement of the cherry trees, for the orchard sloped down sharply to the right from the road. Now I was myself again, and not troubled by the self-possession and silent watching of the world. Only one house was in sight, and only a fragment of that, seen among the fruit trees. I came to a bank in shadow and my quick eye saw among the vetches and weeds a red-ripe wild strawberry. It melted on my tongue, while I looked for others, pushing the grass and leaves hastily aside with hands already drenched with the cold dews. Here was a harvest of which I had not dreamed when I set out. Step by step, searching the bank, I moved on without noticing that I was already descending the hill to-

wards Staplehurst plain, without noticing that the
trees began to close over the road again, shutting
out the sun. Suddenly on the cold air I smelt a hot
sweet smell, and recognized it at once, a sweet brier,
a rarity! I forgot the strawberries and reached up to
find which, among the various wild rose bushes,
bore this delicious scent. I pinched the leaf buds and
smelt them, and found the brier. But at the same
moment, while I gathered a twig to take home, I
caught sight of a gipsy encampment awake and in
full life on a grassy siding, not a hundred yards away.
Two collarless smooth brown dogs were sitting on
the grass with their forelegs outstretched; their eyes
were watching me. Half a dozen children were
watching me; they were wretchedly dirty, bare-
footed and rough-headed—the youngest was a baby
of scarcely walking age, and the eldest a dark fierce-
looking creature, a girl of thirteen or so. The woman
was pushing more sticks on to the fire under the black
soup-kettle, and the new blue smoke was climbing
up past her through the shadow of trees. The man,
ruffianly and sullen, had paused on his way to two
bony horses at graze down the hill, and stood in the
middle of the road looking back at them. There was
no link of humanity between us—these gipsies were,
to me, wild and dangerous creatures of the earth,
thieves and kidnappers, outlaws—and I slid down

through the thick wet grass of the bank and hurried away, frightened to run however, lest running should be a provocation. One of the dogs got up and stretched himself and moved a pace or two in my direction, and the woman turned from her fire to curse him. As soon as they were safely hidden by a bend in the road, I ran on fast into the sunlight, and there I met the bearded imperturbable Mr Brumly trudging down to work through the morning. I knew him for a friend, and oh how relieved I was of my terror of the gipsies when he answered my good-morning kindly and passed me. With him between us I was no longer afraid.

Going home through the morning was a more earthly experience. Two loud gun reports in quick succession and a sudden demoniacal shout: "Hahaha Hoorooahroar!" had no power for terror over me. It was only the cherry-minder at work, scaring the birds from the ripening fruit. After his shout there was the loud rattling and clanging of tins from every part of his orchard at once, as though a small army of boys had suddenly sprung to life there. But I knew the mechanics of this. It was caused by the fellow who had fired the gun and shouted. Under the trees he had hung up bunches of old and battered tins all over the garden, and these were simply connected together by long lines of string, so arranged at last that he had but to pull one string to rattle his tins in all the remote parts of the orchard. This was a noise quite naturally connected in my mind with the hum and song and silence of June. The houses at the Green were now awake. One or two chimneys sent up thin threads of smoke into the sky, as straight as a good sacrifice; Mrs Strange's door stood open, and several labourers passed me on their way to work.

As I turned the corner by the five playground ash trees in sight of home, I met John.

"Is it breakfast-time yet?" I asked him. And as it was not I turned with him.

"Let's go and watch the bird-scarers in Roberts's orchard," I suggested. "The cherries near the road are getting red, and there's gipsies down by the Mallions, and I found a lot of wild strawberries ripe. Lend me your knife," I said, "I want to make a squeaker." So as we sauntered along under the laurels and larches that divided the lane from the Farm, we chose the big white deadnettle stems and slit them and cut them according to an art we cherished, and made the morning hideous with loud and dissonant squeals. In time we reached the cherry orchard fence and hung over it, sucking the deadnettle squeakers, while the cherry-minder fired his muzzle-loader over our heads, or shouted like a giant to frighten the dwarf birds, or pulled that string that filled the acres with the rattle of tins on tins. Birds flew in and out of the orchard over our heads, careless of the dangerous gun; the sun gained rapidly in heat and quickly dried the dew wherever it shone now. We idled on and on in the morning, and at last began to go home to breakfast, sure of our virtue and our pocket-money for that idyllic day.

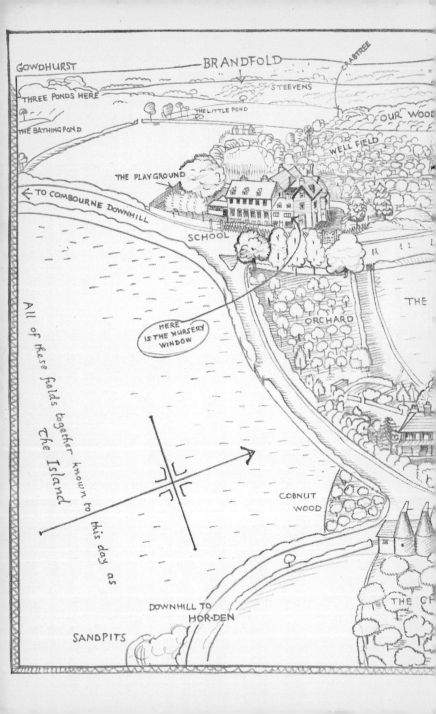

GOWDHURST

BRANDFOLD

CRABTREE

THREE PONDS HERE

STEEVENS

THE LITTLE POND

OUR WOOD

THE BATHING POND

WELL FIELD

THE PLAYGROUND

← TO COMBOURNE DOWNHILL

SCHOOL

THE

ORCHARD

HERE IS THE NURSERY WINDOW

All of these fields together known to this day as The Island

COBNUT WOOD

DOWNHILL TO HOR-DEN

THE C

SANDPITS